WITHDRAWN

The Quest
of Enlightenment

❖ Wisdom of the East Series ❖

The Quest of Enlightenment

*A selection of the Buddhist Scriptures
translated from the Sanskrit by*

E.J. Thomas, M.A., D.Litt.

Charles E. Tuttle Company, Inc.
Boston • Rutland, Vermont • Tokyo

Published in the United States in 1993 by
Charles E. Tuttle Company, Inc. of
Rutland, Vermont & Tokyo, Japan, with editorial offices
at 77 Central Street, Boston, Massachusetts 02109.

Editorial Note © 1992 Charles E. Tuttle Company, Inc.

For reproduction rights, contact the publisher.

Library of Congress Catalog Card Number 93-60006

ISBN 0 8048 1846 0

This is a facsimile edition of the work originally published in London by John Murray in 1950.

PRINTED IN THE UNITED STATES

CONTENTS

CHAPTER		PAGE
	INTRODUCTION	1
I	THE DREAM OF QUEEN MĀYĀ	11
II	THE BIRTH OF GAUTAMA	15
III	THE VISIT OF ASITA	18
IV	THE FOUR SIGNS	22
V	THE GREAT RENUNCIATION	26
VI	THE ENLIGHTENMENT	29
VII	THE FIRST PREACHING	34
VIII	THE NOVICE'S TEN RULES	38
IX	THE EXHORTING OF PŪRṆA	40
X	UPAGUPTA AND VĀSAVADATTĀ	44
XI	THE KING WHO WOULD NOT FIGHT	49
XII	BIRTH-STORY OF BLACKIE	53
XIII	THE MARKS OF NON-SELF	57
XIV	GUPTIKA'S DISCOURSE	60
XV	BIRTH-STORY OF THE EXPULSION OF THE DEMONS	63
XVI	THE FORMULA OF WELFARE	65
XVII	BUDDHA'S LAST MEAL	70
XVIII	THE DEATH OF BUDDHA	74
XIX	THE BODHISATTVA'S VOW	80
XX	QUALITIES OF A BUDDHA	82
XXI	BUDDHA AS SUPRAMUNDANE	85
	INDEX	87

EDITORIAL NOTE

WHEN the Wisdom of the East Series first appeared in the early part of this century, it introduced the rich heritage of Eastern thought to Western readers. Spanning time and place from ancient Egypt to Imperial Japan, it carries the words of Buddha, Confucius, Lao Tzu, Muhammad, and other great spiritual leaders. Today, in our time of increased tension between East and West, it is again important to publish these classics of Eastern philosophy, religion, and poetry. In doing so, we hope the Wisdom of the East Series will serve as a bridge of understanding between cultures, and continue to emulate the words of its founding editor, J. L. Cranmer-Byng:

> *[I] desire above all things that these books shall be the ambassadors of good-will between East and West, [and] hope that they will contribute to a fuller knowledge of the great cultural heritage of the East.*

The Quest of Enlightenment

INTRODUCTION

In the history of Buddhism, a religion which extends from the vihāras of Ceylon and Burma to the prayer-wheels of Tibet and the pagodas of China and Japan, there has been a great gap—the story of its growth in India itself. This gap is now being filled up. It is becoming possible, with the recovery of more and more of the original documents, to show the growth of Buddhism in its Indian home, and to explain the different forms which it has taken throughout the centuries.

An eminent scholar, L. de la Vallée Poussin, has well remarked, " It is necessary to understand that there was never anything like Protestantism in the history of Buddhism." There was never any violent break. Buddhism developed new features without ever discarding the original teaching. We find this teaching embedded in the story of the prince brought up in ignorance of the ills of human life, his revulsion on finding that old age, sickness, and death are the lot of all, his sudden flight from home, his six years of struggle to find a way of escape, and his enlightenment, when " a light went up ", and he saw the truths, which as Buddha, " the Enlightened ", he preached for forty-five years.[1]

This is the legendary setting in which all schools have preserved their doctrines. We find the earliest records of this teaching in the Scriptures preserved in Ceylon. In these we have the only complete form of the Buddha's utterances in an Indian language. But the fact must not be forgotten that the

---

[1] The exact date of his death is uncertain. The Indian schools put it 100 years before Aśoka (accession 269 B.C., coronation 265 B.C.). The Ceylon Chronicles put it 218 years before Aśoka's coronation.

Canon of the Buddhist schools in India was essentially the same. All schools had essentially the same canon, which for long was preserved only by memory, so that variations of expression and arrangement are found, but no differences of doctrine. Doctrinal differences did arise in the schools, but these were expressed in works quite distinct from the original Scriptures, and they are discussed below. It is thus possible to draw up from the Scriptures of the Indian schools an outline of the doctrine, as has been done for the Pāli in the companion volume in this series.[1]

THE SCRIPTURES

The Scriptures of the Indian schools were, like those of the Pāli, arranged in three divisions, the Tripiṭaka, "the threefold Basket".

1. *Vinaya-piṭaka*, the Basket of Discipline. The basis of this is the list of rules for the Order of monks and nuns, recited at the fortnightly meetings of the Order, the four fundamental rules being the forbidding of (1) incontinency, (2) theft, (3) taking life or persuading to suicide, (4) false boasting of supernatural attainments. This portion forms the *Vinaya-vibhanga*. Except for a few minor rules it corresponds closely with the Pāli. It is followed by the *Vinaya-vastu*, giving rules for admission to the Order and regulations for daily life, and there are two supplementary sections. The whole is accompanied by a commentary explaining how the rules came to be laid down, and

---

[1] *The Road to Nirvāṇa*. The language of the Ceylon Scriptures is known as Pāli. It is a middle Indian dialect, and probably close to Māgadhī, the language of Buddha himself. It stands in relation to the Vedic language much as Italian stands to Latin. When the Indian schools consigned their Scriptures to writing they used Sanskrit, a dialect much closer to Vedic, but this Sanskrit shows many traces of having been translated from a popular dialect resembling Pāli.

in this many legends were added. This portion varies very much in the different schools.

2. *Sūtra-piṭaka*, the Basket of discourses. The four divisions, known as *āgamas*, correspond to the first four of the Nikāyas of the Pāli Sutta-piṭaka.

Ekottarika-āgama. One subject in addition. In the first section of this one subject is discussed, in the second two, and so on up to eleven.

Madhyama-āgama. Discourses of medium length.

Dīrgha-āgama. Division of long discourses.

Saṃyukta-āgama. Division of connected discourses.

To these the Pāli adds a fifth division. Although the other schools do not recognize it as such, they possess many of the works which it contains, such as the *Dhammapada* and many Jātakas. But while the Pāli made one work of the birth-stories or Jātakas, the Sarvāstivādins included them in *Avadānas*. These collections of Avadānas (lit. heroic feats), though containing many tales of Buddha's previous births, also give legends of his last life and his prophecies of the future career of disciples. The Mahāsaṅghika school also had an enormous avadāna, the *Mahāvastu-avadāna*, giving the "Great Story" of the life of Buddha in his last existence with many birth-stories and long passages from the Vinaya and Sūtras of this school.

3. *Abhidharma-piṭaka*, the Basket of further Dharma. This like the Pāli consists of elaboration of the doctrines in the discourses, and was developed independently in the different schools. The Sarvāstivādins had seven works, one of which (a list of doctrinal terms) occurs as a discourse among the Pāli suttas.

When the Pāli Scriptures were discovered there was a tendency to set aside all other forms of Buddhism as degenerations. Yet it is clear that when the first Buddhist missionaries planted their doctrines in Ceylon, there was still in India a great body of believers who held exactly the same teaching. This is the Buddhism which continued to grow in India, and from which came the later schools that spread over eastern Asia. Now that their Scriptures are being recovered it is becoming possible to trace the real history of Indian Buddhism.

Although Buddhism claimed to be entirely new, it took over several cosmological Hindu conceptions. The problems that it had to face were thus determined by these presuppositions. One of these was the theory of cycles (*kalpas*). The universe wakes out of its sleep, evolves, reaches a stage of apparent stability, and sinks to rest again. The cycles recur endlessly, and individuals are born and reborn therein according to their karma. Here are two more beliefs that Buddhism took for granted; rebirth and the doctrine of karma, the belief that all deliberately willed actions result in reward or punishment for the actors, if not in this life then in a future existence. For the man who followed the rules of sacrificial brahminism this was the only prospect, endless rebirth and death.

But already there had arisen teachers who proclaimed that they had found a way of escape from this eternal round. The Buddhists refer to them as ascetics (samaṇas) and brahmins. Little is known of them historically, but one of these bodies, the Jains, still exists. Their leader taught the annihilation of karma as the means of release, and this state of release they called Nirvāṇa.

It was among such seekers after final peace that Buddha began his own teaching. The legend tells us that he began with a group of five disciples, who had left the world with him. After practising austerities for six years he found the true way of meditation and won enlightenment. All schools possess what they hold to be the first sermon that he preached when he had discovered the truths (Ch. VII). Doubtless it was repeated many times during his forty-five years of teaching. It was entirely new in proclaiming a " way unheard before ". Beginning by insisting on pain or ill as the fundamental fact of worldly life, it claimed to show its origin and the means or way for its cessation. This way consists in a course of self-training, the Noble Eightfold Way : first a training in morality, followed by repeated meditation on the truths until they are realized with absolute conviction. Then the state of full knowledge results. The disciple has become an arhat (lit. worthy one), and enjoys the peace of Nirvāṇa.

For this training several lives may be needed. The disciple gradually casts off the fetters (vices and false views), which hinder his vision of the truths. When he has realized the truth that all is impermanent he breaks the first three fetters and comes to *Entering the stream*. Further bonds are broken, and he becomes a *Once-returner*, who will be reborn only once more in this world, then a *Non-returner*, who will not be reborn here but in the formless world, and with his last birth he attains Arhatship, consisting in full realization of the truths and the state of Nirvāṇa. But the Sarvāstivādins went further than this. In a discourse which Buddha is said to have preached while on his way to Kuśinagarī (Kusinārā), we are told that " many hundreds of thousands took the formula of refuge (in Buddha, the Doctrine, and the Order), some attained the fruit of Entering the Stream, some the fruit of Once-returner, some the fruit of Non-returner, and some having left the world attained arhatship." But the account continues by saying, " by some the thought of attaining the enlightenment of a disciple was roused, by some that of attaining the enlightenment of a private Buddha, and by some the thought of attaining supreme, perfect enlightenment "—that is to say, the wish to become a perfect Buddha.

There is nothing here out of harmony with the earlier teaching. Buddha himself was said to have begun with the same thought, and as there will be other Buddhas there may be beings now alive in whom the thought has arisen. The Sarvāstivādins developed this teaching in stories of disciples who make the wish to become a Buddha.

In all this there is little room for speculation, and it has even been said that Buddha rejected metaphysics. This loose and misleading statement is due to the fact that he excluded certain definite questions from discussion. These four questions, known as the undetermined questions, are:

(1) Whether the universe is eternal or not.
(2) Whether the universe is finite or not.
(3) Whether the vital principle (*jīva*) is the same as the body.
(4) Whether a released person after death exists, or does not exist, or exists and does not exist, or whether he is neither existent nor non-existent. They were set aside because they do not tend to tranquillity and enlightenment.

On these matters there has been much discussion, and here it is only possible to give the points that may be gathered directly from the texts. It will be seen that the question of the self (*ātman*) is not one of these questions. On this the Buddhists had a definite theory. They analysed the self (not merely the soul but the whole concrete individual) into five groups: the body, feeling, perception, consciousness, and the sankhāras or aggregates, a group which includes all manifestations of will and any other mental feature which may arise. These groups are always changing, but are never entirely dispersed until Nirvāṇa is attained. There is a discourse (see Ch. XIII), on the marks of non-self, which has been held to deny the existence of the self. This is not what the discourse says. It is quite negative, and all that it tells us is that the self is not to be found in any one of the five groups. However, in later parts of the Canon we do find *anattavāda*, the doctrine of non-self. The self that is there denied is the theory of the self as held by brahmins and Jains, the view that behind all the changing mental phenomena there is some permanent entity. But if there is no *ātman* behind the five groups, what happens when they are finally dispersed at the death of the arhat? Some scholars have said, final annihilation. And yet this view was expressly rejected by the Buddhists themselves. There is the story of a disciple who held that "a monk in whom the āsavas are destroyed at the dissolution of the body is cut off and destroyed, and does not exist after death", and he is reproved for his evil view. This view is also rejected in one of the undetermined questions, but in that question about a released person any assertion either positive or negative is also rejected. It is impossible to make any positive statement about the permanent state of Nirvāṇa, as nothing in the world of perpetual change can describe it.

These are some of the doctrines of Buddhism as held by the disciple who has rejected every worldly pursuit in order to devote himself to the one aim of winning true knowledge. At the side of this is usually placed "popular Buddhism". But the real distinction is the Buddhism as carefully taught to the ordained disciple, and the views on Buddhism that any layman might possess. The latter might vary from a mere kindly feeling towards a body of wanderers intent on a non-worldly aim to the earnest desire of the layman who was eager to learn from the discourses of Buddha and his disciples. There can be no doubt that it was the power of Buddha as a popular preacher that led to such wide extension of the doctrine. The immediate aim of the layman was not to find ultimate peace, but to know how to live rightly in the world, and Buddha with his moral earnestness and truly ethical conceptions set before the common man a practical ideal. This is expressed in the ten paths of moral action: refraining from taking life, refraining from taking what is not given, refraining from unchastity, refraining from falsehood, from slander, from harsh language, from frivolous talk, absence of covetousness, absence of malice, right views.

The ten paths are often referred to in the birth-stories and popular tales as being followed by non-Buddhists who lived before the appearance of a Buddha. They show Buddha as a practical instructor starting from the moral conceptions recognized by his hearers, rousing their better impulses, and inspiring them with higher ideals of action. And the tales not only illustrate and set forth noble ideals of virtue, but also emphasize the other side of the truth, which even the evil-doer could not entirely ignore:

> The deeds of mortals perish not,
> Even in a hundred million ages;
> When the fulness of time has come,
> Then do the deeds of men bear fruit.

There are several lists of eighteen schools, but they do not represent the state of the community at any one time, and most of them have disappeared. The most important group was that which developed from the Sarvāstivādins. This name is due to a peculiar theory of the nature of time held by some branches, but it has nothing to do with the doctrine. Their doctrine, as expressed in their Scriptures, was identical with that of the Pāli school. They developed an independent but similar Abhidharma and, as has been shown above, in their avadānas and birth-stories they brought forward the view that a disciple, instead of attaining release under the teaching of a Buddha, might form the wish to become a Buddha, and thus reveal the doctrine to others. This is illustrated in the story of the gardener in Chapter XIX.

INTRODUCTION

A still earlier school was the Mahāsanghika. From this arose the Lokottaravādins, who held that Buddha had attained a stage beyond the ordinary laws of human existence, so that his state was supramundane (*lokottara*), and his apparently human actions merely convention. A poem on the subject has been included in the *Mahāvastu*, and is given in Chapter XXI.

The peculiar doctrines of both these schools were continued by the schools of Mahāyāna, "the great career", which taught (and in China and Japan still teach) that the career of every disciple should be the attainment of Buddhahood. They also developed the Abhidharma doctrine of the impermanence of things into the view that all perceptible objects are "void" or empty of reality, and that their true existence is "suchness", absolute reality, identical with Nirvāṇa and Buddhahood. Yet in all schools there still remains the fundamental teaching, the four truths, the Way, and Nirvāṇa.

Note.—Several terms in the following passages translated from the Sanskrit appear in a slightly different form from the Pāli, such as *arhat, bodhisattva, dharma, sūtra*, which in Pāli would be *arahat, bodhisatta, dhamma, sutta*. Other terms are *Gautama* (*Gotama*), Buddha's clan name, *Kapilavastu* (*Kapilavatthu*) his birthplace, *Kuśinagarī* (*Kusinārā*) the place of his death. *Anāthapiṇḍada* (Anāthapiṇḍaka), p. 80, is the title of the great lay disciple of *Srāvastī* (*Sāvatthī*) meaning, 'giver of alms to the unprotected'.

I. THE DREAM OF QUEEN MĀYĀ

THERE is no continuous life of Buddha in the Scriptures beyond isolated incidents, but a tradition probably existed, as we find the record much the same in all schools. One fragment in verse preserved both in the Pāli and Sanskrit Scriptures gives us the main dates of his life, namely, that he left the world at the age of twenty-nine and died at the age of eighty. See Chapter XVIII. The story extending from his life in heaven before his last birth down to his enlightenment and first preaching belongs in the Pāli to the commentaries. Other schools made it into an avadāna and added it to their Scriptures. Among the Lokottaravādins this was the *Mahāvastuavadāna*, "the Great Story". The *Lalitavistara* "the extended account of the sports (of the Bodhisattva)", from which the following account is taken, is now a Mahāyāna sūtra, but is probably a development of a Sarvāstivādin avadāna.

WHEN the cold season was over, in the month of May (*Vaiśākha*), with the coming of the lunar constellation Viśākha, in the fair season of spring, then the leaves were expanding and the trees were covered with lovely flowers, free from cold and heat, gloom and dust, and the earth was covered with soft grass. At that time the Bodhisattva, chief of the three worlds, the world-honoured, having reflected on the due season, on the full moon of the fifteenth, when his mother had taken the fast-day vows, and when the moon was in conjunction with the constellation Pushya, descended from the Tushita-heaven, mindful and self-conscious in the form of a white elephant. Six-tusked, with crimson head, his tusks lines of gold, complete in all his limbs, he descended into the right side of his mother. Having descended he remained on the right side, not at all on the left.

Queen Māyā having fallen asleep on a pleasant couch beheld this dream:

> Six-tusked, shining like snowy silver,
> Fairfooted, with beautiful trunk and scarlet head,
> To my bosom came a noble elephant
> With sportive gait and joints firm as a thunderbolt.
>
> And never had such bliss been seen
> By me or heard of or experienced,
> As with ease of body and delight of mind
> I was caught in the rapture of meditation.

Now queen Māyā, her dress bedecked with ornaments, glad in body and mind and full of joy, delight, and grace, arose from her noble couch, and accompanied by her train of attendants descended from the top of the noble palace, and went to a grove of aśoka-trees. When comfortably seated in the grove, she sent a messenger to king Śuddhodana: " May the king come, the queen wishes to see you." So king Śuddhodana on hearing the message was delighted in mind, and his body trembled. He rose from his throne, and attended by his ministers, citizens, courtiers, and kinsfolk arrived at the aśoka-grove, but was unable to pass within. He thought that he was too heavy to enter the grove, and standing at the entrance he reflected for a moment, and at that time uttered this verse:

I do not remember that when standing at the head of men mad with battle
My body seemed so heavy as to-day;
This my own family-house to-day I cannot enter;
What can then be here for me? Whom can I ask?

Then the gods of the Pure Abode, showing half their bodies in the sky, addressed the king with a verse:

THE DREAM OF QUEEN MĀYĀ

Endowed with vows, austerity, and virtue, revered in the three thousand worlds,
Full of friendliness and compassion, crowned with merit and knowledge,
The Bodhisattva has descended from the Tushita heaven,
The Great Being, O king, has become thy son in the womb of Māyā.

Joining his ten fingers and shaking his head
The king entered, and was filled with amazement;
Looking at Māyā, who had put aside her pride,
He said, "what can I do, what should be done for you? Tell me."

The queen said:

A Great Being, like snowy silver, brighter than moon or sun,
With fair feet and perfect limbs, six-tusked,
An elephant with joints firm like a thunderbolt, lovely,
Entered my womb; hear the matter.
The threethousandfold universe I beheld clearly shining,
Gods and goddesses in millions sang praises to him lying there;
Nor did I feel any fault or wrath or dulness;
With tranquil mind I knew the bliss of contemplation.
It were well, O king, to summon brahmins swiftly,
Who recite the Vedas in the house and well know the precepts,
To expound this my dream with truth, and tell
What of good it may be to me or of evil to the family.

Hearing these words the king straightway
Summoned brahmins versed in the Vedas and law-books;
Māyā stood forth, and said to the brahmins:
"Of the dream that I have seen hear the matter."

The brahmins said:

Tell, O queen, the kind of dream that was beheld;
When we have heard, then shall we know.

The queen said:

A Great Being, like snowy silver, brighter than moon or sun,
With fair feet and perfect limbs, six-tusked,
An elephant with joints firm like a thunderbolt, lovely,
Entered my womb. Expound the matter.

Hearing these words the brahmins spoke thus:
Receive abundant joy; no evil is there to the family;
Thou shalt have a son, his limbs adorned with the marks,
Sprung from a royal race, a universal king, a great being.
And he, abandoning the realm of the senses,
Shall leave his home, and free from ties, in compassion for the world
Shall become a Buddha, and conspicuous in the three worlds
With the essence of the immortal he shall gladden all the world.

> Having set forth their pleasant speech,
> When they had shared the royal food,
> And taking the gift of royal robes
> The brahmins then set forth again.
>
> (*Lalita-vistara*, 62 [Lef. 54].)

II. THE BIRTH OF GAUTAMA

THE following narrative, like the preceding passage, is from the *Lalita-vistara*. Its chief difference from the Pāli account is in the increased importance given to the bodhisattva. He is not merely born with the thirty-two marks of a Buddha, but is held to have already acquired a Buddha's qualities.

So queen Māyā knowing it was time for the birth of the Bodhisattva, through the wondrous power of the Bodhisattva, in the first watch of the night came to the king, and addressed him in verses:

"Hear me, O king, as I speak what I have thought; suddenly the wish has come to me of going to the park. If it is no displeasure or harm or trouble to you, at once would I go to the garden of sport.

Here you are held by penance with your mind on religion; I have for long been bearing the pure being. The trees have burst into flower, the sāl-trees are in bloom; it is fitting that I should go to the park.

Spring for women is the best season, the time of adornment; humming with bees, resounding with the song of cuckoos; lovely for long has the pollen-dust been floating; good were it to give the order for us to go and delay not."

Hearing these words of the queen the lord of the earth, delighted at heart, said to his attendants: "Harness the chariots with array of horses and elephants; adorn the Lumbinī-grove flourishing in its glories . . ."

Now queen Māyā on reaching the Lumbinī-grove alighted from the splendid chariot attended by divine and human maidens, and wandering from tree to tree, going from grove to grove, looking at tree after tree, came gradually to a magnificent plaksha tree . . . Now the plaksha tree through the wondrous power of the Bodhisattva bent and bowed down. So queen

Māyā like a lightning flash stretched out her right arm and seized a plaksha branch, and stood playfully with open mouth looking at the sky. And at that moment sixty hundred thousand apsarases from the gods of the realm of desire approached to form an escort for queen Māyā.

It was with such a miracle that the Bodhisattva had entered his mother, and at the completion of ten (lunar) months he issued from his mother's right side, conscious and self-possessed, unsoiled by the stains of birth, such as is said of no other, as having the birth-stains of others.

At that moment Śakra, king of the gods, and Brahmā Sahāmpati stood before him. They with supreme reverence, conscious and self-possessed, took the Bodhisattva and with all his limbs wrapped him in a divine kāśika-robe. And the gabled casket in which the Bodhisattva had stayed while in his mother's womb was caught up by Brahmā and the Brahma-gods and taken to the Brahma-heaven as a relic (*caitya*) for the purpose of worship. And further the Bodhisattva was not touched by any human being, but it was the gods who then first touched the Bodhisattva. So the Bodhisattva as soon as he was born came down to the ground. As soon as the Bodhisattva, the great being, touched the earth a great lotus pierced the earth and appeared. Nanda and Upananda, two nāga kings [water serpents], appeared with half their bodies in the sky, created two streams of cold and hot water, and bathed the Bodhisattva. With Śakra, Brahmā and the world-guardians going in front many hundred thousands of other gods bathed the Bodhisattva as soon as he was born with scented water, and scattered flowers over him. In the sky two chowries (fly-whisks) and a jewelled umbrella appeared. Standing on the great lotus he looked round at the four quarters. Looking at the four quarters with a lion's look, the look of a great man, he looked round. Now at that time

THE BIRTH OF GAUTAMA

the divine eye of the Bodhisattva, owing to the ripening of his previous roots of good action, appeared. With his divine eye he beheld all the threethousandfold thousandfold universe with its cities, towns, villages, countries, kingdoms, and capitals, with its gods and men. He knew the mind and action of all beings, and knowing them he looked round and said, " Is there any being who is like me in morality, meditation, and knowledge, or in the practice of the roots of goodness ? " And the Bodhisattva saw no being in the threethousandfold thousandfold universe equal to himself.

(*Lalita-vistara*, 88 [Lef. 78].)

III. THE VISIT OF ASITA

THE story of the sage Asita was widely known, but the details vary much in the different schools. In the *Lalita-vistara* he is said to have lived in the Himalaya, and the account in the *Mahāvastu* here given shows other differences. According to the Pāli he was an ascetic who lived near the king's palace. After his visit he tells his sister's son Nālaka of the approaching advent of a Buddha, and says that when he appears his nephew should abandon the world in his teaching.

The story has been treated as the original of the story of Simeon in Luke, ch. 2, but the differences as well as the resemblances are very striking. In the Gospel the angels were seen by shepherds, and Simeon did not appear till six weeks later, and then not at the boy's house. Simeon departed in peace, but Asita went away with lamentation. Still, among other parallels to the Gospel story this is held to be the most striking.

IN the southern country there was a young brahmin, the son of a brahmin of high family in Ujjenī. He was dark and black of colour, learned, clever and wise. From a family of teachers he had learnt the Vedas, mantras, and law-books. Then with his knowledge of the Vedas he left his house and went to the Vindhya mountain leaving the world and adopting the life of a sage. He ate roots, fruits, and leaves, and lived an austere life. He built a hermitage on the Vindhya mountain, and by the outer Way with practice, effort, and striving he attained the four trances and realized the five higher knowledges. Being learned in these sciences and knowing the Vedas he became widely known and famous as the seer Asita. He went through the air by his great magic power and influence and lived in his hermitage with 500 pupils and Nālaka [his nephew]. Just when the Bodhisattva was born he perceived the earthquake and the light, and heard the lovely superhuman sounds of singing and music, he saw the divine flowers falling, thousands of gods and apsarases with divine scented garlands in their hands going through the air to the east and hundreds of other marvels, and his hair rose with delight. "What has happened to-day in Jambudvīpa? Through whose wondrous power is it that the earth quakes and hundreds of marvels appear?" Thus with his divine eye he saw that in the east in Kapilavastu a son was born to Śuddhodana, meritorious, eminent, of great wondrous power, through the glory of whose wondrous power such hundreds of marvels had appeared in Jambudvīpa. He thought, "At the right time and place I will see the boy." Then knowing the time and occasion for seeing the boy, attended by many pupils he went by magic power through the air, and reaching Kapilavastu came to the door of the women's apartments of king Śuddhodana. The ministers and the doorkeeper seeing the sage rose to meet him. "What does the reverend one command, and what is the purpose of his coming?" The sage said, "Announce to Śuddhodana that the sage Asita wishes to see him." The porter informed the king. King Śuddhodana being informed of the arrival of Asita, the learned, famous, mighty sage, said to the door-keeper, "Let the sage enter." The door-keeper ran and announced to the sage, "Let your honour enter."

The sage entered. The king with his seraglio on seeing the sage rose to meet him. "We welcome the reverend one, let the reverend one sit down." The sage having wished the king success in victory sat down. The king asked, "What, reverend one, is your purpose in coming?" The sage said, "I wish to see your boy." At that time the boy had attained a certain calm trance. They thought the boy was asleep. Then the king said, "Come in a short time, the boy is now asleep." The sage said, "O king, the boy is not asleep." The king turned to the boy and saw that he was awake. The king amazed at the sage said, " The sage has great power," and gave the command to bring the boy to the sage. The boy on a robe of soft antelope-hair was brought to him. The sage even from a distance seeing the marks of a great man on the boy's body clasped his hands on his head and rose to meet him, and having done reverence to him he took the boy. The sage observed the boy's thirty-two marks of a great man. He had heard in the palace the word " universal king ". The interpreters of signs had said, " The boy will be a universal king." The sage thought, " He will not be a universal king, he will be a Buddha in the world, and I in no long time shall end my life, and I shall not see this jewel, I shall not hear his doctrine, and shall not see his excellent company." He wept and shed tears. King Śuddhodana with his seraglio seeing the sage Asita weeping became anxious. " Why, reverend one, on seeing the boy do you weep ? Surely you do not see any misfortune for him ? When the boy was born the earth quaked in six ways, a light appeared in the world, he was worshipped by thousands of gods, there were showers of divine flowers, and thousands of musical instruments gave forth sounds. When the boy was born 500 boys in Kapilavastu were born and 500 girls, 500 male and 500 female slaves were born, 500 elephants and 500 horses ; 500 stores of treasure appeared, 500 kings sent wishes for success in victory, and other marvels occurred. And yet on seeing the boy the reverend one weeps. Tell me, reverend one, surely you do not see any misfortune for the boy." The sage said, " I see no misfortune for the boy. At some time, O king, and in some place there is the appearance of such great men. This great man has appeared, he will be a Buddha in the world, and I being old shall not see him. He will preach his noble doctrine that leads to peace and Nirvāṇa, and I shall not hear it. I shall not see his excellent company, I shall not see the Buddha's miracles. It is, O king, because I see this great misfortune for myself that I weep." The saga having by four causes prophesied with certainty that he would be a Buddha in the world, departed.

(*Mahāvastu*, ii. 30.)

IV. THE FOUR SIGNS

OF the events between the birth of the Bodhisattva and his leaving the world we have no real knowledge. His mother is said to have died seven days after his birth, and he was brought up by his aunt Prajāpatī. He received the name Siddhārtha (Pāli, Siddhattha), "he who has accomplished his aim". From the Scripture we learn that he was brought up very delicately, and this according to the legend was because of the prophecy of the brahmins at his birth that he would become either a universal king or a Buddha. Hence he was kept by his father without the knowledge of old age, sickness, and death, until at the age of twenty-nine he was shown the four signs.

THE Bodhisattva decided that he would go into the park. King Śuddhodana ordered his ministers to keep watch between the palace and the park . . . and by the king's orders the ministers set watch on the road, and placed men at each point so that no old man or sick man or blind . . . should appear before the prince as he went to the park . . . Ghaṭikāra the potter, who had been born as one of the gods of the Pure Abode, and others of those gods created the form of an old man before him, aged and advanced in years, white-haired, his body marked with spots, broken, bent forward, leaning on a staff, and going with tottering limbs. The Bodhisattva on seeing him asked the charioteer, "Who is that man so strange, old, advanced in years . . . going with tottering limbs?" The charioteer said, "Prince, what has that question to do with you? The man is called old, with his body exhausted by age. We are going now to the park, sport and delight and play with the five pleasures of sense." The prince said, well, tell me, are all too liable to old age and subject to the law of old age? When the old age of a being that is born is known, what pleasure does a wise man take in it? Turn the chariot round, charioteer, enough of going to the park."

The prince having turned back entered the house. King Śuddhodana asked the ministers why the prince had turned back and had not gone to the park. The ministers said, "O king, the prince saw an old man and turned back, and no more wanted to go to the park." The king said, "May it not be as it was prophesied by the sage Asita. It will be a good thing to make the prince sport and delight and play with dancers, singers, and musicians, so that he may like to stay in the house." The concerts in the prince's seraglio were like those in the world of the gods, but his mind was not on concerts; he thought about the old man.

[In exactly the same way the prince's later excursions are described, when he sees a sick man and a corpse.]

The prince said, "Well, charioteer, will this man never more see his father or mother or brother or sister or his kinsfolk and friends?" "Yes, prince, nevermore . . ."

The prince said:

"Death to thee and me is equal, neither enemy nor friend;
 Like the season he advances, hard to conquer or control.
 Not the families of lowly or of highborn does he count;
 Fearless like the sun in heaven, there he marches on his way."

The charioteer said:

"Pleasures, success, and kingly weal, delight, good fortune,
 Ask about them, the chiefest things in all the world;
 What hast thou to do with seeing death, the dreadful,
 The root of pain and ills, mankind's destruction?"

The Bodhisattva said:

"He that has seen an old man, sick man, corpse,
 And does not shudder in this world of change,
 Should be deplored, for he, the senseless one,
 Is like a blind man on the high road lost."

The prince said: "well, charioteer, we too are liable to death and subject to the law of death. When the old age, the sickness, the death of a being that is born is known, what pleasure does a wise man take in it? Turn the chariot round; enough of my going to the park."

[The prince pays a fourth visit to the park, and the gods show before him one who had left the world, wearing yellow dress, with tranquil senses, and composed gait, looking half a fathom in front of him.]

The prince asked him, "noble one, why have you left the world?" The wanderer said, "for the sake of subduing and calming myself and attaining Nirvāṇa.[1] On hearing the wanderer's words he was pleased . . .

Mṛigī, the Śākya lady, was the mother of Ānanda. When she saw the prince going out of Kapilavastu in such glory and magnificence she praised him with a verse:

> Happy (*nirvṛto*) indeed is thy mother,
> And happy too is thy father;
> Happy too is the woman,
> Whose husband thou shalt be.

The Bodhisattva hearing the word 'nirvāṇa' was pleased with nirvāṇa, and stopped and seized it.

> Hearing the sound of nirvāṇa
> He gave ear to nirvāṇa;
> Having beheld supreme Nirvāṇa
> He meditated on the place of safety.

---

[1] *Nirvāṇa*, 'state of happiness', but as there are two roots from which the word may be formed it may also mean 'extinction'; and the participle *nirvṛto*, 'having attained happiness or extinction'. The prince plays upon the two meanings of the word.

THE FOUR SIGNS

As the prince meditated on nirvāṇa, he took no notice of the Śākya lady Mṛigī, and did not speak to her, and then she became sad. "From among such a multitude has the prince been praised by me, and I have not even been noticed by him."

[*Mahāvastu*, ii, 150.)

V. THE GREAT RENUNCIATION

ACCORDING to the Pāli account the Bodhisattva returned from his fourth visit to the park, when he saw the man who had left the world, and made the Great Renunciation the same night. In the *Mahāvastu* his father decides to make him crown prince. In both accounts his renunciation was made on his becoming disgusted with his seraglio. On the same night, according to the Pāli, his son Rāhula was born, but according to the *Mahāvastu* he was then conceived, i.e. he descended like Buddha himself from the Tushita heaven into his mother. This feature may be due to the docetic character of the *Mahāvastu*, which made Buddha's earthly acts mere appearance, so that his behaviour as a human being was adopted only " to conform to the custom of the world ".

RĀHULA having descended from the Tushita heaven passed into his mother's womb at midnight. The Bodhisattva on awaking saw his seraglio asleep, one holding a lute, one a flute . . . one a drum, one with her hand on her neck, one with a tabor on her head, two with their heads in each other's laps, one with her limbs thrown right and left, one with spittle flowing from her mouth. The Bodhisattva seeing them thus lying separately on the ground thought the seraglio was like a cemetery. He got up from sitting cross-legged, and moved aside the fine cotton curtains of the apartment. Chandaka was stationed as his attendant. " Chandaka, bring me the horse Kanthaka." Chandaka said, " prince, it is midnight, what is the use of a horse at this time and place ? Your palace is like Vaiśravaṇa's heaven, enjoy it, what do you want with a horse at this time and place ? Your seraglio is like a host of apsarases, enjoy it. What do you want with a horse ? " Many such things Chandaka said . . . The prince said, " Chandaka, I want a horse now, bring

THE GREAT RENUNCIATION

me Kanthaka." Chandaka thought, "as the prince at this time and place asks for Kanthaka while the people are happily asleep, he now wants to renounce the world." So then, while he was harnessing Kanthaka, with a loud voice he uttered a cry so that the king should awake and the people and all Kapilavastu. The gods sent a deep sleep on all the people within and without. Kanthaka also, when he was being brought neighed with a loud neigh (thinking), "at the sound of my neighing king Śuddhodana and the people will wake," but though the sound went a league all round it was not noticed, and no one awoke. Many thousands of gods surrounded Kapilavastu and with scented garlands did honour to the Bodhisattva as he renounced the world. [Many marvels and miracles of the gods are here omitted.]

The Bodhisattva attended by thousands of gods and the four great kings went south from Kapilavastu for twelve leagues to the town Anomiyā, not far from the hermitage of the sage Vasishṭha. There the Bodhisattva and Chandaka stopped. The Bodhisattva put his ornaments into Chandaka's hand, entrusted to him the horse Kanthaka and the royal umbrella for his father Śuddhodana, and gave a farewell to Mahāprajāpatī Gautamī and all his relatives (saying), "when I have done what has to be done I will come back as the turner of the Wheel of the Doctrine" . . .

The Bodhisattva thought, "what of the going forth and the topknot?" With a sword he cut off his topknot, and when cut off it was taken by Śakra king of the gods and worshipped in the heaven of the Thirty-three, and the Topknot-festival was held. Kanthaka licked the Bodhisattva's incomparable feet. The Bodhisattva taking no notice went on . . .

Chandaka was sent back by the Bodhisattva when he renounced the world from the town of Anomiyā and Chandaka and Kanthaka came to Kapilavastu . . . When Chandaka entered the palace royal excellent food and drink was brought to him, and to Kanthaka sweets mixed with honey were brought, and other royal food was set before him, but he would not eat . . . Through grief for the Bodhisattva he took no food, and he died on not seeing the Bodhisattva. On his death king Śuddhodana with great royal magnificence did reverence to his body, and he was at once reborn in the heaven of the Thirty-three as the god named Kanthaka.

(*Mahāvastu*, ii. 159.)

VI. THE ENLIGHTENMENT

AFTER the Great Renunciation Gautama is said to have spent six years in search of a way of release from the ills which he had suddenly found to be involved in worldly life. During these years he was attended by five disciples, who left him when he discarded his methods of severe austerity. Then having found the true way of meditation, he took his seat under a pipal tree and won enlightenment.

Apart from its legendary setting the account is of the highest importance in illustrating some of the chief Buddhist doctrines. The four trances show one of the methods of meditation by which the mind is concentrated and removed from outer influences. The divine eye and memory of past existences are two of the powers of a Buddha, but they are acquired in some degree by all arhats. The final stage is the destruction of the three corruptions, whereby full knowledge is attained.

The Chain of Causation is a detailed exposition of the cause of pain shown by the passing of the individual from birth to birth. Through ignorance he passes to a new birth, and then in the form of rebirth-consciousness passes to another birth, develops mind and body, the six senses, contact, feeling, craving, grasping and the desire of becoming. This leads to another birth and again to old age and death.

THE FOUR TRANCES

THUS the Bodhisattva having routed the opposition of Māra and crushed his enemy, victorious in the forefront of the battle, with parasol, banner, and standard raised, attained the first trance, which is free from sensual desire and wicked and evil ideas, is accompanied with reasoning and investigation, arising from seclusion and full of joy and pleasure, and abode in it. With his mind fixed on one point he attained the second trance, which is without reasoning and investigation, arises from concentration, and is filled with joy and pleasure, and abode in it.

Abiding with equanimity towards joy and aversion, mindful and conscious he experienced bodily pleasure, what the noble ones describe as abiding with equanimity, mindful and happy, he attained the third trance, which is without joy, and abode in it. With the abandoning of pleasure and pain, even before the disappearance of elation and depression, he attained the fourth trance with equanimity and mindfulness purified from pain and pleasure, and abode in it.

THE DIVINE EYE

So the Bodhisattva with divine eye, purified beyond human sight, saw beings passing away and being reborn, of good or bad colour, of good or bad destinies, low or high, going according to their karma. He understood: alas! these beings who have led evil lives with misdeeds of body, with misdeeds of speech and mind, speaking evil of the noble ones, holders of false views, these who acquire karma through their false views, at the dissolution of the body after death, which ends in a state of misery and suffering, are reborn in the hells. But those beings who have led good lives with good deeds of body, with good deeds of speech and mind, who are of right views, they on account of the karma due to their right views on the dissolution of the body with a happy destiny are reborn in the heavens. Thus with divine eye, purified beyond human sight, he saw beings passing away, being reborn of good or bad colour, of good or bad destinies, low or high, suffering according to their karma. Even so the Bodhisattva in the first watch of the night realized knowledge, dispelled darkness, and produced light.

MEMORY OF PAST EXISTENCES

So the Bodhisattva with thus concentrated mind, purified, cleansed, brilliant, spotless, with the defilements gone, supple, dexterous, firm, and impassible, in the middle watch of the night drew out and directed his mind to realizing knowledge and insight into the memory of his former existences. He remembered many kinds of former existences of himself and others, one birth, two, three, four, five, ten, twenty, thirty, forty, fifty births, a hundred, a thousand, a hundred thousand, many hundred thousands, many crores, hundreds of crores, thousands of crores, ten thousands of crores, hundreds of thousands of crores, many hundreds of thousands of ten thousands of crores, up to a cycle of evolution of the universe, a cycle of dissolution, a cycle of evolution and dissolution, many cycles of evolution and dissolution. There was I, of such and such a name, clan, caste, colour, livelihood, length of life, suffering such pleasure and pain. Passing away thence I was reborn there, passing away thence I was reborn here. Thus did he remember the many kinds of former existences of himself and all beings with their special modes and details.

THE CHAIN OF CAUSATION AND ENLIGHTENMENT

The Bodhisattva thought: wretched verily is this world, in that beings are born, grow old, die, pass to another existence, and are born again. And moreover they know no escape from all this great mass of pain with old age, sickness, death and so forth. Alas! no ending is known of all this great mass of pain, with all this old age, sickness, death, and so forth.

Then the Bodhisattva thought: when what exists do old age and death exist, and by what are old age and death conditioned? He thought: when birth exists old age and death exist, for old age and death are conditioned by birth.

Again the Bodhisattva thought: when what exists does birth exist, and by what is birth conditioned? He thought: when becoming exists birth exists, and rebirth is conditioned by becoming.

Now the Bodhisattva thought: when what exists does becoming exist, and by what is becoming again conditioned? He thought: when grasping exists becoming exists, for becoming is conditioned by grasping.

Now the Bodhisattva thought: when what exists does grasping exist, and by what is grasping conditioned? He thought: when craving exists grasping exists, for grasping is conditioned by craving.

Again the Bodhisattva thought: when what exists does craving exist, and by what is craving conditioned? He thought: when feeling exists craving exists, for craving is conditioned by feeling.

Again the Bodhisattva thought: when what exists does feeling exist, and by what is feeling conditioned? He thought: when contact (of the senses) exists feeling exists, for feeling is conditioned by contact.

Again the Bodhisattva thought: when what exists does contact exist, and by what is contact conditioned? He thought: when the six sense-organs exist contact exists, for contact is conditioned by the six sense-organs.

Again the Bodhisattva thought: when what exists do the six sense-organs exist, and by what are the six sense-organs conditioned? He thought: when mind and body (name and form) exist the six sense-organs exist, for the six sense-organs are conditioned by mind and body.

Again the Bodhisattva thought: when what exists do mind and body exist, and by what are mind and body conditioned? He thought: when consciousness exists mind and body exist, for mind and body are conditioned by consciousness.

Again the Bodhisattva thought: when what exists does

consciousness exist, and by what is consciousness conditioned? He thought: when the aggregates (elements of the individual) exist consciousness exists, for consciousness is conditioned by the aggregates.

Again the Bodhisattva thought: when what exists do the aggregates exist, and by what are the aggregates conditioned? He thought: when ignorance exists the aggregates exist, for the aggregates are conditioned by ignorance.

[This is the Chain in reverse order (from effect to cause). He then repeats it in direct order, then negatively in reverse order.]

At that time, monks, I duly knew: this is pain, this is the cause of pain, this is the cessation of pain, this is the Way. I duly knew: these are the corruptions, this is the cause of the corruptions, this is the cessation of the corruptions, this is the Way that leads to the cessation of the corruptions. I duly knew: this is the corruption of sensual desire, this is the corruption of desire for becoming, this is the corruption of ignorance, this is the corruption of false views. Here the corruptions cease without a remainder.

Even so, monks, in the last watch of the night . . . everything that with noble knowledge was to be known, understood, attained, seen, and realized by a man . . . by the Bodhisattva with full knowledge was embraced in one moment of thought. Supreme, perfect enlightenment was won, and the threefold knowledge was attained.

(*Lalita-vistara*, ch. 22.)

VII. THE FIRST PREACHING

THE account of Buddha's enlightenment is much enlarged in the commentaries and later literature by the story of his victory over Māra, the chief god of the realm of sensual desire. It has little importance except as being symbolical of Buddha's escape from the power of the senses. After staying seven weeks near the Bodhi-tree he received food from two travelling merchants, and decided to preach. His two former teachers, to whom he thought of imparting his knowledge, were dead, but by his Buddha-eye he knew that his five former disciples were at Benares, and there he preached his first discourse, the setting in motion the Wheel of the Doctrine.

The discourse gives in outline the essentials of the positive teaching of Buddhism—the four truths, the fourth truth of which is the Noble Eightfold Way, which by a course of morality and meditation leads to full knowledge.

THE five monks of the Bhadra-group, Ājnātakauṇḍinya, Aśvaki, Bhadraka, Vāshpa, Mahānāman were dwelling in the Rishipatana.[1] The Lord having gone out of Benares after collecting his alms and finishing his meal went to the Rishipatana. The five saw the Lord. On seeing him coming from afar they decided on their behaviour. "This ascetic Gautama is coming, he is slack, he lives in abundance, and has given up striving. No one ought to get up." The Lord came, and they did not remain in their places. Just as birds in their nests or on a bough fly up when fire from below heats them, even so the five monks, as he came from afar, finding no pleasure in their seats, rose up and went to meet the Lord. "Come, friend Gautama, welcome, friend Gautama, greeting to friend Gautama." The Lord said,

[1] The deer-park at Benares. It occurs below as Rishivadana and in Pāli as Isipatana.

"you have broken your agreement, monks. Do not, monks, greet the Tathāgata with the word 'friend'." Then when the Lord addressed them with the word 'pupil', all their marks as brahmin students, their dress and behaviour, at once disappeared, and they appeared in the three robes with shining bowls, with hair arranged naturally,[1] and their gait was as if they were monks of a hundred years standing. This was the ordination of leaving the world of the five monks. [The narrative is broken here, and the First Sermon follows as it would appear in its place in the Canon.]

Thus have I heard: at one time the Lord was dwelling at Benares, at Rishivadana in the deer-park. Then the Lord addressed the five elders: "Monks." "Lord," the monks replied to the Lord. The Lord said to them: There are these two extremes, monks, for one who has left the world. What are the two? The one, devotion to lusts and pleasures, vulgar, belonging to the common people, ignoble and purposeless, does not tend to a completely religious life, to disgust, absence of passion, to the state of ascetic, to enlightenment, to Nirvāṇa; and the other, devoted to self-mortification, painful, ignoble, purposeless. These, monks, are the two extremes of one who has left the world, and the Tathāgata by avoiding both these extremes has through enlightenment in the noble Doctrine and Discipline attained the Middle Path, which produces insight, tends to calm, and leads to disgust, absence of passion, cessation, to the state of ascetic, to enlightenment, to Nirvāṇa. And what, monks, is the Middle Path . . . won by the Tathāgata? It is the Noble Eightfold Path, namely, right view, right resolve, right effort, right action, right livelihood, right speech, right mindfulness, right concentration. This, monks, is the Middle

---

[1] The *Lalita-vistara* says their hair was cut, which would be the natural state for a monk.

Path in the noble doctrine and discipline won through enlightenment by the Tathāgata, which produces insight, tends to calm, and leads to disgust, absence of passion, cessation, to the state of ascetic, to enlightenment, to Nirvāṇa.

Now, monks, there are these four Noble Truths. What are the four? The Noble Truth of pain, the Noble Truth of the cause of pain, the Noble Truth of the cessation of pain, and the Noble Truth of the Path that leads to the cessation of pain.

Herein, monks, what is the Noble Truth of pain? It is, birth is pain, old age is pain, sickness is pain, death is pain, union with unpleasant things is pain, separation from pleasant things is pain, not getting what one wishes and pursues is pain; the body is pain, feeling is pain, perception is pain, the mental elements are pain, consciousness is pain, in short, the five groups of grasping are pain. This, monks, is the Noble Truth of pain.

Herein, what is the Noble Truth of the cause of pain? It is craving, tending to rebirth, combined with delight and passion, and finding delight here and there. This, monks, is the Noble Truth of the cause of pain.

Herein, what is the Noble Truth of the cessation of pain? It is the complete and trackless destruction, cessation, abandonment, relinquishment, and rejection of that craving which tends to rebirth and finds delight here and there. This, monks, is the Noble Truth of the cessation of pain.

Herein, what is the Noble Truth of the Path that leads to the cessation of pain? It is the Noble Eightfold Way, namely, right view, right resolve, right effort, right action, right livelihood, right speech, right mindfulness, right concentration. This, monks, is the Noble Truth of the Path that leads to the cessation of pain.

This is pain: as I reflected, monks, on doctrines unheard

before, knowledge arose, insight arose, intelligence arose, wisdom arose, light appeared.

This is the cause of pain: as I reflected . . . wisdom arose, light appeared.

This is the cessation of pain: as I reflected . . . wisdom arose, light appeared.

And this is the Path that leads to the destruction of pain: as I reflected . . . wisdom arose, light appeared.

Again, I must comprehend the Noble Truth of pain.

As I reflected . . . wisdom arose, light appeared.

Again, the Noble Truth of the cause of pain must be abandoned: as I reflected . . . wisdom arose, light appeared.

Again, the Noble Truth of the cessation of pain must be realized: as I reflected . . . wisdom arose, light appeared.

Again, the Noble Truth of the Path leading to the cessation of pain must be practised: as I reflected . . . wisdom arose, light appeared.

As long, monks, as I did not with due wisdom truly comprehend these four Noble Truths with the three sections and twelve divisions, so long I did not understand with full enlightenment, nor did knowledge arise in me, nor was my steady release of mind realized. But when, monks, with due wisdom I truly comprehended these four Noble Truths with the three sections and twelve divisions then I understood that I was enlightened with full enlightenment, knowledge arose in me, and my steady release of mind and release of wisdom was realized.

(*Mahāvastu*, iii. 328.)

VIII. THE NOVICE'S TEN RULES

THE admission of Buddha's son Rāhula to the Order is said to have taken place on the occasion of a visit of Buddha to his home. The admission was the ceremony of leaving the world (*pabbajjā*), when the candidate becomes a novice, and is placed in the care of a tutor. At the age of twenty he may receive full ordination (*upasampadā*). It will be seen that the first five rules are also the rules for laymen. On the fast-day the layman also keeps the first nine rules, rules seven and eight being combined, so that they form the eight fast-day rules of the layman.

THE Lord then addressed the elder Śāriputra : " Admit Rāhula to the Order, Śāriputra, he will have the same hut as yourself." The elder then asked the Lord, " How, Lord, shall I admit him ? " The Lord said, " As the admission of a youth in the noble doctrine and discipline. Say [i.e. tell Rāhula to repeat] ' I, Rāhula, go for refuge to the Buddha, I go for refuge to the doctrine, I go for refuge to the Order. A second time I, Rāhula (say), Buddha is my refuge, no other is my refuge. The doctrine is my refuge, no other is my refuge. The Order is my refuge, no other is my refuge. I, Rāhula, as long as I live will refrain from taking life ; as long as I live I will refrain from taking what is not given ; as long as I live I will refrain from unchaste lusts ; as long as I live I will refrain from lying ; as long as I live I will refrain from liquor and strong drink that are occasions of intoxication. As a layman I will abide by these five precepts.

I, Rāhula, leave the world after the Lord Buddha, who has left the world. A second time, I leave the world after the Lord Buddha, who has left the world. A third time, I have left the world after the Lord Buddha, who has left the world. I,

Rāhula, as long as I live refrain from taking life with the abstaining of the precept of a novice, down to [1] I hold the precept not to accept gold and Śilver. These are the ten precepts." Then the elder removed Rāhula's hair, ordained him, Śāriputra took him by his right hand, and Maudgalyāyana by his left, and they set him on a grass mat.

(*Mahāvastu*, iii. 268.)

---

[1] This is a phrase which implies an abbreviation. The omitted items are, 2–5 of the layman's precepts as above, and 6–9 of the novice's precepts, (6) not to eat at the wrong time (after noon), (7) not to see dancing and singing, (8) not to use garlands, scents, unguents, or adornments, (9) not to use a high or large bed.

IX. THE EXHORTING OF PŪRṆA

THIS discourse as well as the following one are a refutation of the charge sometimes made against the arhat ideal that it is a selfish one. From the first the disciples were exhorted to go preaching for the good of many. Pūrṇa, though he was only beginning his course in the religious life, decided to go as a missionary in a savage border country, and during his preaching there won arhatship.

In the next tale Upagupta, though still a layman, goes to speak to Vāsavadattā about the true nature of the body, and when he sees her ghastly state realizes the truth so clearly that he reaches the stage next to arhatship.

THE elder Pūrṇa approached the Lord, and having saluted him with his head stood on one side. Standing on one side the elder Pūrṇa said to the Lord, " It would be well for me if the Lord would so teach me the doctrine shortly that having heard it shortly from the Lord I may abide secluded, earnest, zealous, with myself controlled ; that I may go forth for the sake of which noble youths remove their hair and beard, put on yellow garments, and with right faith go forth from a house to a houseless life, to that life which ends in the highest religious life, having in this actual life known, realized, and attained (the truth) that my rebirth is destroyed, the religious life has been led, done is what was to be done, I know that there is no becoming beyond this."

Thereat the Lord said to the elder Pūrṇa, " Good, Pūrṇa, good indeed is it, Pūrṇa, that you say that. Therefore, Pūrṇa, listen well and carefully, and bear it in mind. I will speak : there are forms to be recognized by the eye, desirable, agreeable, pleasing, attractive, rousing passion, and exciting. If a monk on seeing them approves and welcomes them and clings to them and continues to cling, as he does so enjoyment arises, and from enjoyment delight and satisfaction arise. When there is delight and satisfaction passion arises, and when there is delight and passion the fetter of delight and passion arises. A monk, Pūrṇa, who is bound by the fetter of delight and passion is said to be far from Nirvāṇa. There are, Pūrṇa, sounds recognized by the ear, scents recognized by smell, tastes recognized by the tongue, tangible things recognized by the body, and mental things recognized by the mind, desirable, agreeable, pleasing, attractive, rousing passion, and exciting. When a monk sees them and welcomes them, he is said to be far from Nirvāṇa. (If a monk on seeing them does not approve . . . the fetter of delight and passion does not arise[1]) and he is said to be very near to Nirvāṇa. You have been incited, Pūrṇa, by this concise exhortation. Where do you wish to live and take up your abode?" "Incited by this concise exhortation, Lord, I wish to live and take up my abode in the districts of the Śroṇāparāntaka people." "The Śroṇāparāntaka people, Pūrṇa, are passionate, they are violent, cruel, reviling, furious, and abusive. If the Śroṇāparāntaka people meet you with evil, false, harsh speech and revile and are furious, and abuse you, what will you think?" "If so, Lord, I shall think, 'Really the Śroṇāparāntakas are good, really they are kind that meet me only with evil, false, harsh speech and are reviling and furious, and abuse me, and do not strike me with their hands or with clods.'" "The Śroṇāparāntakas, Pūrṇa, are passionate . . . If they strike you with their hands or with clods, what will you think?" "If they do so . . . I shall think, 'Really the Śroṇāparāntakas are good, really they are kind that they strike me with their hands or clods and not with sticks or knives.'" "The Śroṇāparāntakas, Pūrṇa, are passionate . . . If they strike you with sticks or

[1] This is supplied from the Tibetan version.

knives, what will you think?" "If they do so ... I shall think, 'Really the Śroṇāparāntakas are good, really they are kind that they strike me with sticks or knives, but do not entirely deprive me of life.'" "The Śroṇāparāntakas, Pūrṇa, are passionate ... If they entirely deprive you of life, what will you think?" "If the Śroṇāparāntakas do entirely deprive me of life, I shall think, 'There are disciples, Lord, who are distressed about this foul body, they want to get rid of it, and in disgust take a knife or swallow poison or die by using a rope or fall from a cliff. Really the Śroṇāparāntakas are good, really they are kind who free me with such little trouble from this foul corpse.'" "Good, good, Pūrṇa, equipped with that patience and goodness you can live in the districts of the Śroṇāparāntakas and take up your abode there. Go, Pūrṇa, being released release (others), having crossed over take (others) across, being consoled console, and having won Nirvāṇa cause (others) to win Nirvāṇa."

So the elder Pūrṇa approving and welcoming the Lord's words saluted the Lord's feet with his head and went away. So the elder Pūrṇa at the end of that night dressed himself early, took his bowl and robe, and went into Śrāvastī for alms. After collecting his alms and having had his meal he returned. Collecting the bed and seat that he used, and taking his bowl and robe he went journeying to the Śroṇāparāntaka districts and reached them. Then dressing himself in the morning he took his bowl and robe and went into Śroṇāparāntaka for alms. A certain hunter with bow in hand was going hunting and saw him. He thought, "This wretched shaven ascetic that I have seen is unlucky," and loading his bow and drawing it back to his ear he rushed after him. The elder Pūrṇa saw him, and thereupon drew back his outer robe, and said, "Good fellow, I have come in for a purpose hard to fulfil. Strike here." And he spoke this verse:

THE EXHORTING OF PŪRṆA

For the sake of which birds enter the snare, and deer are caught in the net,
And armed with arrow and pike and lance men perish for ever in war,
And fish in the water wretched and pitiful swallow the hook that is set,
For that same sake with evil of belly have I come here from afar.

He reflected, "This wanderer, endowed with such patience and goodness, why should I kill him?" So thinking he became kindly disposed. Then the elder Pūrṇa taught him the doctrine and established him in the formula of taking refuge (in Buddha, the Doctrine, and the Order), and converted 500 laymen and 500 lay women. He had 500 vihāras built furnished with beds, chairs, stools, couches, pillows, and cushions. At the end of three months he realized in himself the three knowledges and became an arhat, free from passion for existence in the three worlds.

(*Divyāvadāna*, 37.)

X. UPAGUPTA AND VĀSAVADATTĀ

THE following tale is part of the *Aśokāvadāna* or life of Aśoka, which is partly given in the *Divyāvadāna*. Upagupta, a perfume-seller's son, afterwards entered the Order, became a great preacher, and chief adviser of the emperor Aśoka.

IN Mathurā there was a courtesan named Vāsavadattā. Her maid used to go to Upagupta to buy perfumes, and Vāsavadattā said to her, " girl, the perfume-seller must be in love with you, you bring so many perfumes." The girl said, " noble lady, Upagupta, the perfume-seller's son, is full of beauty, he is full of amiability and sweetness, and he does his business honestly." When Vāsavadattā heard that, a feeling of passion for Upagupta arose. Then she sent her maid to Upagupta with the message, " I want to come to you and make love with you." So the maid gave Upagupta the message. Upagupta said, " It is not the time, sister, for me to see you." Vāsavadattā bestowed her favours at the price of 500 purāṇas,[1] and the thought occurred to her that he was not able to give 500 purāṇas, so she sent her maid to Upagupta saying, " I don't want even a kārshāpaṇa from the noble one, I only want to make love to him." The maid gave the message thus, and Upagupta said, " it is not the time, sister, for me to see you." Then a certain son of a guildmaster went to visit Vāsavadattā, and a certain merchant from the North bringing 500 horse-loads arrived at Mathurā. He asked who was the principal courtesan, and learnt that she was Vāsavadattā. He took 500 purāṇas and went to see Vāsavadattā. Thereupon Vāsavadattā moved by greed, after turning out the guildmaster's son and throwing him into a privy, made love with the merchant.

[1] The purāṇa was a gold coin and the kārshāpaṇa of copper.

UPAGUPTA AND VĀSAVADATTĀ

Then the guildmaster's son on getting free informed the king. The king thereupon said, " go, sirs, cut off Vāsavadattā's hands and feet, ears and nose, and leave her in a cemetery," and this was done.

Then Upagupta heard that Vāsavadattā had had her hands, feet, ears, and nose cut off, and had been left in a cemetery. The thought came to him, " Before now she wanted to see me for sensual reasons, but now that her hands, feet, ears, and nose have been cut off, now is the time to see her."

And he said:

> When in splendid garments her limbs were robed,
> And with lovely adornments she was bedecked,
> Better was it for those that aim at release
> And are averse to rebirth, that they should not see her.

But now:

> This is the time to see her, when her pride and passion and glee are gone,
> When with a sharp sword she has been ruined, and her body appears in its true form.

So accompanied by a boy attendant he took his umbrella and with tranquil gait reached the cemetery. Her messenger-girl out of affection for her former state was standing near and keeping off the birds and other creatures. She informed Vāsavadattā, saying, " Noble lady, Upagupta, to whom I was sent by you again and again, has arrived; he must have come because he is pained by lust and passion." Vāsavadattā on hearing that said:

> With my beauty destroyed, suffering pain,
> Lying on the ground, and stained with blood,
> When in this state he beholds me,
> How can he have lust and passion?

Then she said to the messenger-girl, "Collect the hands and feet, the ears and nose that were cut from my body." So she collected them and hid them with a cloth, and Upagupta came and stood before Vāsavadattā. Then Vāsavadattā seeing Upagupta standing before her said, "noble sir, when my body was flourishing and fit for sensual enjoyment, then I sent a messenger again and again to the noble sir, and he replied, 'it is not time, sister, for me to see you', and now when my hands and feet, ears and nose, have been cut off, and I am lying in my blood and filth, why have you come now?

And she said:

> When this my body was fair as the heart of a lotus,
> Adorned with costly robes and ornaments,
> And when indeed it was worthy to be seen,
> Then you were not seen by me of little good fortune.
> Now what is it that you have come to see,
> When my body is not worthy to be seen?
> Gone is the wonder of its grace, delight, and glee,
> Dreadful is it, and smeared with blood and mud.

Upagupta said:

> Not, sister, because pained by passion
> Have I come here into your presence;
> But to see the impurity of lusts
> And their true nature have I come here.
> Though hidden by your robes and ornaments,
> By your outward charms that dispose to lust,
> Yet when examined by the strenuous
> Not as such would you be seen.
> But this your body is to be seen,
> Here in its true nature free from artifice;
> Ignorant and blameworthy are they
> That take delight in this common carcase.

UPAGUPTA AND VĀSAVADATTĀ

> In this body, bound with skin and soaked in blood,
> Covered with hide, overspread with masses of flesh,
> All overlaid with a thousand veins,
> Who verily would delight in it, and why?

And further, sister:

> When he sees forms of fair outside,
> The ignorant man delights in them;
> But knowing their inner foulness
> The wise man finds in them no pleasure.
> Cast away is the impurity
> Of a corpse that has been cast away;
> The pure withdraw from lusts,
> The lustful look upon them as pure.
> But they that hear the sweet voice
> Of the All-enlightened One, and act,
> Abandon lusts that cause distress and grief and pain,
> Which are ever censured by the good.
> With minds freed from the causes of lust
> They have gone to the tranquil forest;
> They go to the further side of the great ocean of becoming
> Making use of the raft of the Way.

Vāsavadattā on hearing this was roused from worldly existence, and through reflecting on the Buddha's virtues her heart was moved, and she said:

> Even so is all this,
> As you say, O learned one;
> Having obtained you, good one,
> Have I heard the Buddha's word.

Then Upagupta gave Vāsavadattā a graduated discourse, and expounded the Truths. And Upagupta having grasped the true nature of Vāsavadattā's body reached absence of passion for the realm of desire. Through his own teaching of the doctrine together with his penetration of the Truths he attained the fruit of Non-returner, and Vāsavadattā attained the fruit of Entering the Stream.

Then Vāsavadattā on perceiving the Truths said with affection to Upagupta :

> Through your support the dreadful way of woe,
> Full of many evils, has been shut ;
> Opened is the meritorious way to heaven,
> And the way to Nirvāṇa have I won.

And further : I go to the Lord, the Tathāgata, the Arhat, the perfect Buddha as a refuge, and to the Doctrine and Order of Bhikkhus." And she said :

I proceed for refuge to him with eye
Pure as a newly opened lotus,
To the passionless Conqueror together with
The [Doctrine] the producer of immortal wisdom, and to the Order.

Then Upagupta having instructed Vāsavadattā with a discourse on the Doctrine went away, and not long after he had gone Vāsavadattā died, and was reborn among the gods. The deities announced in Mathurā that Vāsavadattā having heard the teaching of the doctrine from Upagupta had seen the Noble Truths, and had been reborn among the gods. And the people dwelling in Mathurā on hearing this did worship to her body.

(*Divyāvadāna*, 352.)

XI. THE KING WHO WOULD NOT FIGHT

THE sermon on the Mount says, "resist not evil" (Matt. v. 39). The word for "evil" may be masculine, and the Revised Version translates it, "him that is evil". The principle involved is the same, and there is a tale in the Pāli (Jāt. 51) of a king who refused to fight, and yet was victorious, and recovered his kingdom. The following tale deals with the same problem. In both cases the king was Buddha in one of his former births.

LONG ago in the far past there was a king of Kośala, virtuous, of great eminence, great power, great wealth, and with a great force of chariots. His kingdom was thriving, it was prosperous, peaceful, and wealthy, populous, with happy inhabitants, free from dacoits, robbers were well-controlled, and trade flourished, as he protected it in righteousness. In many a country the fair report of the king's fame went forth, he was honoured as a bestower of alms, he was ready to behave kindly to others, and had a regard for the next world. Thinking that he was righteous the king of Kāśī, who had no regard for the next world, was eager to attack the Kośala kingdom, and having equipped a fourfold army of elephants, horses, chariots, and infantry reached the Kośala country. By means of the Kośala king's ministers with a hired force the Kāśī king was defeated and his whole army put to flight. After a time he came with a stronger fourfold force, and was again defeated. Again and again he came with his army into the Kośala country. Thereby many thousands of living beings on both sides fell by sword, arrow, spear, and lance, and met with disaster. The Kośala king being righteous, compassionate, and regardful of the next world, seeing the thousands of beings that had met with disaster, was agitated in mind, and realized that it was through greed of a kingdom that such unrighteous destruction of life was done. In his agitation he quitted his kingdom and alone without a companion went in disguise to the south, and there by some trade got his living.

As he was going wearied by the journey and suffering from wind and sun, he sat under the cool shade of a banyan tree resting himself, and a merchant engaged in sea-trade, who had lost his ship with the destruction of all his wealth in the sea, was coming from the south from the sea to Kośala. He had heard that the Kośala king was righteous and compassionate, ready to act kindly towards others, that he supported many thousands who had fallen and who had lost their wealth, and furnished them with money, and he thought that the king would give him money so that he could do business and raise himself from his fallen state. Having hopes in the Kośala king he was going by stages from the south and had reached the Kośala king's country. There he met the Kośala king under the banyan tree. The king asked the merchant, " Good brother, don't go on while you are weary and tired, the shade of this banyan is cool, and you are tired with the journey." He replied, " Good brother, good luck to you, I must go." Then the king said, " Good brother, where are you hurrying, and what is your intention in going that you don't wish to rest?" He replied, " Good sir, I am a merchant from a certain city, engaged in sea-trade, and from my city taking various wares with much wealth to the seaports I crossed the great ocean in a well-fitted ship. Then on the great ocean my ship loaded with wealth was wrecked, and I barely escaped alive from the sea on a plank. I am going to the Kośala king to ask for money, whereby I can carry on my trade again and raise myself from my fallen state. It is with this hope that I have come from far and am going there."

Then the Kośala king hearing the merchant's words wept and shed tears. The merchant said, "Good sir, why are you weeping?" The king said, "I am weeping because you having lost your ship have come from far with your hopes on me, thinking that the Kośala king will furnish you with money so that you can carry on your trade again and raise yourself from your fallen state. The Kāśī king has overrun my kingdom, and I have escaped with my bare life to the south, where I shall make a livelihood by some trade. So I am weeping that you on the report of me should have come so far, and that such a misfortune as mine should destroy your hopes." Then the merchant addressed the king in a verse:

> "Through the fame of thee, hero of bounty,
> On hearing of it have I come here from afar;
> My desires were fostered with the strength of hope;
> My hopes have become hopeless on beholding thee."

The king said:

> "I am the bestower of hundreds of desires;
> In the world of men and gods is none like me;
> For thy sake will I sacrifice my life;
> Let not the fame of me be false."

Then the king consoled the merchant, who in despair had fallen on the ground. "You have come here from afar with your hopes fixed on me. I will act for you so that your coming will not be fruitless. For your sake I will sacrifice myself. Bind my arms behind me, and take me to the Kāśī king. Then the Kāśī king will be pleased with you and give you much money. Willingly do I sacrifice myself, and let not the hopes that you had in me be fruitless. Then the merchant said:

> "I cannot to such a hero of men
> Do such a sin for the sake of wealth;
> As is thy fame, even so is it on seeing thee;
> Most hard is that to do, O world-sage."

The king said:

> "What is the worth of life to them
> That have no fame or fortune in the world?
> As in search of wealth thou hast come here,
> Do not return with all thy wishes lost.
> Willingly from foes will I suffer fearful smiting;
> Willingly shall the foe cut up my body;
> Willingly will I undergo the keenest suffering;
> Pain will I suffer; let not thy hopes be vain."

Now the Kāśī king had no pleasure in the life of the Kośala king, and he daily made a proclamation that whoever should bring him the head of the Kośala king, should receive from him a great reward. So as the Kośala king again and again insisted on it, he was bound by the merchant with his arms behind him and brought before the Kāśī king. The Kāśī king said, "Aha, here is the king, a hero and a good fighter, how have you bound him and brought him?" When the merchant had told everything about the reason for his coming, the Kāśī king in astonishment said, "it is not proper for us to deprive such a righteous king of his kingdom," and then he consecrated the Kośala king again in his kingdom, and went away to his Kāśī realm. Thereafter the Kośala king bestowed much wealth on the merchant.

(*Mahāvastu* iii. 349.)

XII. BIRTH-STORY OF BLACKIE

When Buddha was practising austerities during his six years' striving, it was reported to his father that he was dead. This his father refused to believe, owing to the prophecy of the brahmins. The following birth-story was told to show how in his previous life as Blackie his father also refused to believe that his son was dead.

The tale illustrates the general Indian belief in a "truth-utterance". If a wish is made along with an assertion of the absolute truth of a certain fact, not even the power of the gods can prevent the wish being accomplished.

Once in the far past in the city of Benares in the Kāśī country there was a certain brahmin. For forty-eight years he practised celibacy and studied the Vedas. Then thinking it would not be right not to leave offspring he took a wife, and having raised offspring thought that having enjoyed human pleasures it was time to leave the world. He told his wife, and she said, "Who will look after your son or who will look after me? If you intend to leave the world I too will do so, I too will do austerities, I too will practise celibacy." The brahmin said, "Be it so, do you too leave the world." Then they left Benares. On the slope of the Himalaya is a hermitage named Sāhanjanī. There a great sage named Gautama dwelt with 500 pupils, who had acquired the four trances and the five higher knowledges[1]. The brahmin with his wife went there, and abandoned the world under the sage Gautama. His wife too abandoned the world. Then he built a hut of grass and one of leaves near the hermitage with one for his wife Pāragā, and practising by the outer way realized the trances and the higher knowledges ... They

[1] *Abhijñā.* The divine eye, the divine ear, knowledge of others' thoughts, memory of one's previous existences, and psychic or magic power. These may be obtained by "the outer way", i.e. by non-Buddhists. To these the Buddhists added a sixth, destruction of the āsavas, to be acquired only by the Noble Way.

thought, "What shall be the boy's name?" and they said, "The boy is black (*śyāma*), let him be called Blackie (Śyāmaka). So the name Blackie was given him by his parents.

There the boy was brought up in the hermitage. When he could run about, he played with the young deer. Sages practise friendliness, and the birds and deer do not fear them. The hermitage was graced with thousands of deer and birds. When the young deer drank from their mothers' breasts, then Blackie did so also. So he grew up playing with the deer and the birds . . . He collected the roots and the fruits in the hermitage, and offered them to his father and mother. He brought water and sticks and erected huts of grass and leaves, sprinkled and swept the hermitage, and attended on his parents with the greatest respect. Then they grew old and weak and blind, and unable to get their food. He fulfilled all their needs and then attended to himself . . .

Accompanied by deer and birds, by gods, nāgas and fairies he took a pitcher and went to fetch water from a mountain stream. The Kāśī king Peliyaksha was hunting a deer, which disappeared in a thicket. He heard the sound of Blackie, and thinking it was the deer he shot his poisoned arrow and hit Blackie in the heart. The boy put the pitcher down and uttered pitiful cries, "Deer and boars are killed for their flesh, lions, tigers, and leopards are killed for their skins . . . but what could be done with my flesh or skin . . . and with one arrow three people have been killed." The king arrived, and finding him lamenting and weeping was terrified. He leapt from his horse and falling at Blackie's head said, "Thinking it was a deer I shot in ignorance, and I implore your pardon, but why did you say that three have been killed with one arrow? The reverend one is not threefold. How were three people killed with one arrow?" Blackie said, "O king, my mother and father are old and weak and blind, and I am their supporter. I do everything for them, and when I am killed they are killed also. When I am dead there is no life for them. That is why I said that three were killed with one arrow." The king said, " I will lay aside my royal splendour, and will take care of your mother and father. As you have cared for them, so will I do." The boy said, " You have removed the arrow of grief from my heart. As you have promised, so do to my mother and father. It will be a great blessing to you, O king. In order to support the reverend ones you will take this pitcher and go by that path and give them my greeting : Blackie sends his greeting, and says, your only son is dead, and this should not be a cause of grieving and weeping. Everyone in the world of living beings must die. To abide is impossible, and cannot be gained by weeping and grieving, nor can one escape one's own karma. Death is not mine alone, but belongs to all beings. Therefore grieve not, sorrow not. From all dear and pleasant things there is change and deprivation.[1] According to your true promise, O king, do to the reverend ones as you say." Thus having admonished him the boy died.

The king seeing the boy dead wept and lamented. Wiping his tears and taking the pitcher he went to the hermitage by the way that he had been shown. As soon as the king had set off, the boy's body was attended by deer and birds, making a great lamentation. His parents hearing the sound thought, " Never before have we heard such sounds, can it be that Blackie has been hurt by a lion or a tiger or some other wild beast ? " The king reached the hermitage, and the deer and birds raised fearful cries. The sages were still more alarmed. The king tied his horse to a branch, and taking the pitcher

[1] This sentence is the utterance of Buddha, which was repeated by Mahā-Kassapa to the monks after Buddha's death.

approached the boy's parents, saying, "I salute you reverend ones." They said, "Who are you?" [The king explained who he was, and they told him that Blackie was coming with water. The king wept, gave the boy's message, and explained how he was killed.]

The king fell at their feet and besought their pardon. "I will give up my realm and people, and support you here as Blackie did." Then they said, "O king, we are blind and not able to go to the place without a guide. Lead us, O king, to the place where Blackie is. We will raise him up with a truth-utterance, and destroy the poison." Then placing their hands on the king's shoulder they went to the place. Clasping Blackie's head his mother Pāragā stroked his face with her hand and wept and lamented, "The hermitage will be empty deprived of Blackie. The woodland deities lamenting will go away, and the deer and birds not seeing Blackie will go away lamenting." The sage said, "Pāragā, do not weep, do not grieve. What good will weeping and grieving do? We who have followed celibacy with long-practised austerity are able to raise him up with a truth-utterance. I make this truth-utterance, wherewith we shall destroy his poison and bring back his life." Then by this truth-utterance the poison was destroyed: "As you, my son, have never thought anything bad, and have had a friendly mind to all creatures, so may your poison be destroyed. As you have never sought food for yourself without first giving it to your parents, so may your poison be destroyed. As you have ever kept the moral rules towards your parents, so may your poison be destroyed." Then the boy through the wondrous power of the truth-utterance of his parents and his own well-practised power, as a man who has been asleep wakes up, so he gave a yawn and arose.

(*Mahāvastu*, ii. 209.)

XIII. THE MARKS OF NON-SELF

In the Pāli Scriptures is a discourse known as *the marks of non-self*, which appears in the *Mahāvastu* divided into two, as given here. It would be quite natural that when it was given on different occasions it might be so divided. The subject has been discussed in the Introduction. Here it need only be noted that the subject is not the question of the soul, but of the self, the whole individual consisting of the body and the four immaterial parts, and it is denied that the self is to be found in any one of them. Attempts that have been made by Western scholars to prove that the discourse implies the annihilation of the individual at death or at Nirvāṇa are futile, as that was a view always rejected by the Buddhists.

I

The Lord dwelt at Benares, teacher of gods and men. There the Lord addressed the five elders of the Bhadra-group. "Body, monks, is without self; feeling, perception, the other mental elements, and consciousness are without self. If, monks, this body were the self the body would not be liable to sickness and pain, and the production of pleasure in the body would thrive (if I said) may my body be so, may it be not so; and because the body is not the self therefore it is liable to sickness and pain, and the production of pleasure does not thrive in it (if I say) may my body be so, may it be not so. [The same statements are made for the other groups, feeling, etc.]

Therefore, monks, thus you must learn: whatever body there is, internal or external, coarse or fine, base or lofty, far or near, past or present or future, all that body is not mine, I am not that, that is not the self, even so is it to be viewed with right wisdom. Whatever feeling, perception, mental elements, consciousness there is, whether internal or external, coarse or fine, base or lofty, far or near, past or present or future, all that is not mine, I am not that, that is not the self. Even so is it to be viewed in truth with right wisdom."

Thus spoke the Lord while dwelling at Benares in the Rishivadana in the deer-park, and when this exposition was being uttered the mind of the elder Ājñātakauṇḍinya was released from the corruptions (*āsavas*) without clinging (to existence), and in the four (other) monks, the elders Aśvaki, Bhadaka, Vāshpa, and Mahānāman, the pure and spotless eye of the doctrine concerning things was purified, and in thirty crores of gods the pure and spotless eye of the doctrine concerning things was purified. Enraptured the five elders of the Bhadra-group applauded the utterance of the Lord.

II

The Lord, the all-enlightened, addressed the five elders of the Bhadra-group : " If you think, monks, from what root do grief, lamentation, suffering, sorrow, and despair arise, what is their origin and beginning ? " Thereat the elders said to the Lord, " Things have their root in becoming, Lord, they are led from becoming, they have their origin and production in becoming. It were well if the Lord would set forth this matter to the monks. When the monks face to face with the Lord have heard and face to face have grasped it, then in reality they will understand it." Thereat the Lord thus spoke to the five of the Bhadra-group :

" Grief, lamentation, suffering, sorrow, and despair arise from the body as the root, they have their origin and beginning in the body. From feeling as the root, from perception, from the aggregates, and from consciousness arise grief, lamentation, suffering, sorrow and despair, having (therein) their origin and

THE MARKS OF NON-SELF

beginning. Would you think, monks, that body is permanent or impermanent?" "Impermanent, Lord." "Now, monks, when you know the impermanence of body, its unsteadiness, its perishableness, its changing, passing away, and ceasing, those corruptions (*āsavas*) that arise on account of body, which are destructive, distressing, feverish, defiling, which lead to renewed existence, to birth, old age, and death in the future, cease. With their cessation the corruptions will not arise. [The same statement is made of feeling, perception, the aggregates, and consciousness.] Therefore, monks, you should learn: that whatever body there is, internal or external, gross or subtle, low or eminent, far or near, past, future, or present, all this body is not mine, not this am I, not this is the self. Thus, monks, you should learn. [Repeated for the other constituents.] Even so is it to be looked upon in reality with right wisdom." Thus said the Lord while dwelling at Benares in the deer-park Rishivadana, and when that exposition was being spoken the elder Ājnātakauṇḍinya attained mastery of the powers. The minds of the four monks, Aśvaki, Bhadraka, Vāshpa, and Mahānāman, were released without clinging from the corruptions.

(*Mahāvastu*, iii. 335 ff.)

XIV. GUPTIKA'S DISCOURSE

THE discourse of Guptika makes use of the doctrine of non-self to emphasize the complementary truth of the permanent state. Everything that arises must pass away, but beyond this continual change is the permanent state of Nirvāṇa.

Two further points in the doctrine of karma are also illustrated. However much the individual may change from its former state it is still causally linked to the individual that it was when it performed its deeds, so that the same being that performed them suffers for them. Nor does the winning of release require or depend upon the exhaustion of karma. Guptika, though an arhat, was still suffering from a disease and reaping the fruit of his past actions.

THE friends of the elder Guptika came to him and said, " what, elder, is of perishable nature, or what is there in the world of imperishable nature?" "Body, friends, is of perishable nature; with its cessation Nirvāṇa is of imperishable nature. Feeling, perception, the mental elements, and consciousness, friends, are of perishable nature. With their cessation Nirvāṇa is of imperishable nature. What do you think, friends, is body permanent or impermanent?" "It is impermanent." "Again, is that which is impermanent painful or not painful?" "It is painful." "Again, would the learned noble disciple look upon what is impermanent, painful, and liable to change as himself, saying this is mine, I am this, this is my self?" "No, reverend Guptika." [The same argument is given for the other elements.] "Therefore now, whatever body past, present, or future, internal or external, coarse or subtle, base or lofty, far or near, all that is not mine, I am not that, that is not my self, even so is this to be looked at with right wisdom. Whatever feeling there is, perception, mental elements, consciousness, past, present, or future, internal or external, coarse or subtle, base or lofty, far or near, all that is not mine, I am not that, that is not my self, even so is this to be viewed with right wisdom. The learned disciple who thus views feels disgust for body, feeling, perception, the mental elements, and consciousness. Having become disgusted he is free from passion, having become free from passion he is released. The knowledge and insight that he is released arises, 'destroyed is my rebirth, the religious life has been led, done is what was to be done, no other existence (becoming) beyond this do I know'."

Now when this was being spoken, in those friends arose the pure, spotless eye of the doctrine concerning things. The doubts of the monks were roused, and they asked the Lord Buddha, the cutter of all doubts. "What actions, Lord, had been done by Guptika that his body became full of a loathsome and evil-smelling disease, and what action had he done that he became of keen and sharp intellect, and on leaving the world realized arhatship?" The Lord said: Guptika, monks, in former births has done and heaped up actions; who else will suffer for them? Actions, monks, done and heaped up are not ripened in the external earth-element nor water nor fire, nor air, but in the *skandhas*, *dhātus*, and *āyatanas* [1] that have been acquired, both good and bad actions.

> "The deeds of mortals perish not
> Even in a hundred million ages;
> When the fulness of time has come,
> Then do the deeds of men bear fruit."

[Buddha then tells a tale of Guptika's previous life as a guild-

---

[1] The *skandhas* are the five groups of the self as given in the discourse. The *dhātus* (elements) and *āyatanas* (bases) are more elaborate subdivisions of the same groups.

master, when he illtreated a rival, hence his disease; but he afterwards repented and atoned for his crime, and hence his quick attainment of arhatship. He still had to experience the results of both kinds of action.]

(*Avadāna-śataka*, No. 96.)

XV. BIRTH-STORY OF THE EXPULSION OF THE DEMONS

The following birth-story appears to have been invented merely to form an introduction to the Formula of Welfare which follows (Ch. XVI). It illustrates the Buddhist belief that by "the outer way", as practised by non-Buddhists, many of the attainments of Buddhist ascetics may be obtained. See note, p. 53.

When the Lord Buddha crossed the boundary into Vaiśālī, all the demons fled. The multitude was delighted, and said to the Lord, " See, Lord, how when the Lord crosses the boundary of Vaiśālī all the demons flee." The Lord said, what is wonderful, Vāsishṭhas,[1] that when the Tathāgata, after attaining full enlightenment and having become god beyond the gods, has crossed the border of Vaiśālī, all the demons should flee ? On another occasion also, when I was a sage in the city of Kampilla and crossed the boundary, all the demons fled." The Licchavis said, " Another, Lord ? " The Lord said, " Another also."

In the far past, in the Pānchāla country, in the city of Kampilla, there reigned a king Brahmadatta. He ruled his people well and was given to hospitality. His land was thriving, prosperous, peaceful, and wealthy, populous, with happy inhabitants, free from dacoits and robbers, and flourishing with trade. Now the son of Brahmadatta's family priest was named Rakshita. He was distinguished, and had undertaken the ten paths of good action. Perceiving the wretchedness of lusts and understanding a way of escape his mind was much agitated, and he was intent

[1] This is the clan name of the Licchavis of Vaiśālī, so named from a Vedic sage, just as all of Buddha's clan were named Gautamas from another Vedic sage.

on renunciation. As he saw the wretchedness of lusts, he went out to the Himalaya and adopted the wandering life of a sage. Then in the Himalaya he built a hermitage, made a hut of grass and leaves, and lived on roots, leaves, flowers, and fruit. By the outer way he spent the former and latter part of the night in the practice of watchfulness, attained the four trances, and realized the five higher knowledges. Then having attained these the young man lived in the exercise of the ten paths of good action, lived a celibate life, sat cross-legged in his hermitage, and touched the disc of the moon and sun with his hand. He even controlled the gods of the Brahma-world, such was his extreme austerity and great power.

At one time in the great city of Kampilla and the country round a grievous disease due to demons broke out. Afflicted by that demonic disease many thousands of people fell victims to it. King Brahmadatta seeing the great misfortune to Kampilla sent a message to Rakshita in the Himalaya, "In Kampilla such a disease due to demons has broken out, and many thousands of people have fallen victims to the disease. It were well if the Lord would show compassion and come to Kampilla." The sage on hearing the messenger's words came from the Himalaya and reached Kampilla. On the sage crossing the boundary of Kampilla all the demons fled. Then the sage in Kampilla gave a Formula of Welfare, and taught the ten paths of good action to 84,000 people. [Two other birth-stories of the same purport follow.]

So the Lord by gradual stages reached Vaiśālī. Then the Lord in Vaiśālī pronounced the Formula of Welfare both of the inner and outer way. [This is given in the next chapter.]

(*Mahāvastu*, i. 283.)

XVI. THE FORMULA OF WELFARE

This formula occurs in a simpler form in the Pāli Scriptures, where it is known as the Jewel-discourse (*Ratana-sutta*). It forms part of a collection of similar spells still used in Ceylon. Apart from its use as a spell it has an interest as being a kind of creed, belief in the three Jewels, the four stages of progress (each being divided into two, the Way and the Fruit), the need of confession, and the extinction of rebirth with the winning of Nirvāṇa.

REVERENCE to Buddha, reverence to enlightenment,
Reverence to the Freed, and reverence to freeing,
Reverence to knowledge, and reverence to the Knower,
To him supremest in the world pay reverence.

All spirits whatever that are here assembled,
That haunt the earth or through the air are passing,
May all those spirits be well-disposed and kindly,
May they hear welfare uttered by the Victor.

Whatever jewel is in this world or elsewhere
Or any precious treasure in the heavens,
In no wise is it equal to the Buddha,
The god beyond the gods, the man supremest.
In the Buddha is this jewel of perfection ;
So through this truth to us may there be welfare,
Whether from men or superhuman beings.

[Destruction, passionlessness, the immortal, perfect,
Attained by the Śākya-sage in contemplation.]
In the Buddha is this jewel of perfection ;
So through this truth to us may there be welfare,
Whether from men or superhuman beings.

That pureness by the best of Buddhas lauded,
The contemplation called uninterrupted,
Nought is there equal to that contemplation.
In the Doctrine is this jewel of perfection;
So through this truth to us may there be welfare,
Whether from men or superhuman beings.

The persons eight, they that are ever lauded,
Who form four pairs, worthy are they of offerings,
So has the Blessed One declared them worthy,
Of great fruit are the gifts to them presented.
In the Order is this jewel of perfection;
So through this truth to us may there be welfare.
Whether from men or superhuman beings.

All they indeed who thus attain to insight
Three things cast off entirely and abandon:
False theory of a self, uncertainty,
And all there is of ceremonial practice.
In the Order is this jewel of perfection;
So through this truth to us may there be welfare,
Whether from men or superhuman beings.

Whatever act of wickedness the learner
In deed or word or thinking has committed,
Impossible for him is its concealment,
For them that have seen the path impossible.
In the Order is this jewel of perfection,
So through this truth to us may there be welfare,
Whether from men or superhuman beings.

THE FORMULA OF WELFARE

Even as a pillar at a city's threshold
Stands firm in the earth, by the four winds unshaken,
So, I affirm, is the good man unshaken,
Who in the Noble Truths is well instructed,
And pondering the meanings deep perceives them.
In the Order is this jewel of perfection;
So through this truth to us may there be welfare,
Whether from men or superhuman beings.

Who to the Noble Truths apply themselves,
The Truths well taught by the profoundly wise one,
They, even though they be exceeding slothful,
Not to the eight rebirths will be subjected.
In the Order is this jewel of perfection;
So through this truth to us may there be welfáre,
Whether from men or superhuman beings.

They who apply themselves with mind well-purposed,
Renouncing all in Gautama's instruction,
Their end attained, are plunged in the immortal,
Their minds released, delighting in Nirvāṇa.
In the Order is this jewel of perfection;
So through this truth to us may there be welfare,
Whether from men or superhuman beings.

The old is destroyed, the new is not assembled,[1]
Released from becoming are they in the future,
Their seeds destroyed, not sprouting forth again,
Like to an oil-lamp are the wise extinguished.
In the Order is this jewel of perfection;
So through this truth to us may there be welfare,
Whether from men or superhuman beings.

[1] Birth and rebirth.

As when a fire flames up, and then sinks down,
Blazes, and lacking fuel dies once more,
Even so the meditating sons of Buddha,
Seizing the dire results of lust with wisdom,
Depart, not theirs to see the king of Death.
In the Order is this jewel of perfection;
So through this truth to us may there be welfare,
Whether from men or superhuman beings.

In the hot season, in the spring month of Chaitra,
As in a forest grove with tops in flower,
Blown by the wind the branches waft their sweetness,
So do the meditating sons of Buddha
Endowed with virtue waft abroad their sweetness.
In the Order is this jewel of perfection;
So through this truth to us may there be welfare,
Whether from men or superhuman beings.

All spirits whatever that are here assembled,
That haunt the earth or through the air are passing,
To you may human kind be ever friendly,
And day and night for you set forth their offerings.
Therefore be you unwearied to protect them,
Even as a mother pitying her infant.
So through this truth to us may there be welfare,
Whether from men or superhuman beings.

In these, Vipaśyin, Śikhin, Viśvabhū,
Krakucchanda, Kanakamuni, Kāśyapa,[1]
And Gautama, the Śākya-sage, the famous,

---

[1] The six previous Buddhas, with emendation of the text.

THE FORMULA OF WELFARE

Through these the Buddhas of mighty psychic powers
May all the deities be well-disposed;
May they protect us mightily, and furnish
This welfare to the race of human beings.
Therefore be ye unwearied to protect them,
Even as a mother pitying her infant.
So through this truth to us may there be welfare,
Whether from men or superhuman beings.

Him who has overcome the world, and turneth
The wheel of the Doctrine, pitying all beings,
Even such a one, of gods and men supremest,
The Buddha I revere, may there be welfare;
The Doctrine I revere, may there be welfare;
The Order I revere, may there be welfare.

(Mahāvastu, i. 290.)

XVII. BUDDHA'S LAST MEAL

In the Pāli story of Buddha's last meal he is said to have eaten *sūkara-maddava*. This is not the usual word for boar's flesh, but the earliest commentators understand it in this sense. However, they also mention other views, one being that it was a kind of mushroom. There was no religious reason why it should not have been boar's flesh, as meat was allowed, provided that the recipient had not seen, heard, or suspected that it was intended specially for him. In the following Sarvāstivādin account from the Chinese there is no mention of the kind of food, but in another version there is an addition after the statement about the meal: " Chunda had especially cooked sandal-mushrooms, which were looked upon by all the world as a wonderful rarity, and offered these only to the Lord. The Lord said to Chunda, ' Give not of these mushrooms to the monks.' Chunda accepted the order, and did not venture to give them." This does not settle the question as to what the food really was, but only shows that the Chinese translator understood it in the same sense as some of the Pāli commentators.

The following account also includes a discourse to Chunda. It occurs as a separate discourse in the Pāli, and appears to have been inserted here by an editor who thought this the appropriate place for it. In the prose Dr. E. Waldschmidt's version [1] from the Chinese has been followed, but the discourse has been taken direct from the Pāli.

THEN Buddha having early robed himself took his bowl and went with the great Order to the meal (given by Chunda). Buddha and the Order sat on the appointed seats. When Chunda saw that all had taken their places, he took the foods with his own hands and set them before Buddha and the noble Order. At that time there was an evil monk, who then stole a copper bowl by hiding it under his armpit. Buddha by his psychic power caused it not to be seen by the people. Only

[1] *Beiträge zur Textgeschichte des Mahāparinirvāṇasūtra.* Göttingen, 1939.

BUDDHA'S LAST MEAL

Buddha and Chunda saw the wrong deed. When Chunda perceived that Buddha and the Order were fully satisfied, he caused pure water, powder, and tooth-sticks to be passed round, and after they had laid their bowls aside and had washed and rinsed their mouths, then Chunda took a low seat, sat down before Buddha, and reverently questioned the Lord with a verse:

> I ask the recluse, the sage of mighty wisdom,
> Buddha, Lord of the doctrine, free from craving,
> Best of men, the supreme of charioteers,
> How many ascetics in the world are there?, deign to tell.

The Lord replied with a verse, and said:

> Four ascetics there are, no fifth is there,
> Asked as a witness do I make clear to thee:
> He who has won the Way, who shows the Way,
> Who lives in the Way, and he who defiles the Way.

Chunda asked further:

> Whom do the Buddhas call the winner of the Way?
> How is he that ponders the Way incomparable?
> Tell at my asking, who lives in the Way?
> Likewise make clear to me the Way-defiler.

The Lord answered:

> He who has passed beyond doubt, who is free from grief,
> Delighting in Nirvāṇa, released from hankering,
> Leader of the world with its gods and men,
> Such, say the Buddhas, is the winner of the Way.

> Him who here knowing the highest as the highest,
> Announces and expounds even here the doctrine,
> Cutter of doubts, a recluse, and free from lust,
> Him as the second they call the shower of the Way.

Who in the well-expounded words of doctrine
Lives in the Way, restrained and contemplating,
Blameless courses regarding and pursuing,
Him as the third they call the liver in the Way.

He who counterfeits the conduct of the virtuous,
Boastful, a corrupter of homes, and reckless,
Hypocrite, unrestrained, a chatterer,
Seemingly virtuous, he is the Way-defiler.

He who has comprehended this, the layman,
The learned, the noble, wise disciple,
Knowing that all these are not what they seem,
Thus he perceives, and so his faith fails not;
For how the corrupted with the uncorrupted,
The impure with the pure can he confound?[1]

Whereby that stupid man commits an evil deed
He causes doubt all round among the good;
Trust not on outer signs, when one before thee stands,
Depend not on him after short acquaintance.
Common men often make fallacious show,
And ever through the world they go deceiving.

Even as an earring overlaid with gold,
But underneath is copper, base and worthless,
One who is false within, but seeming real,
Draws to him pupils and misleads the good.

At this time the Lord seeing the bounty (of the meal offered by Chunda) set forth his merit in a verse:

[1] Here the Pāli discourse ends.

Of him who gives the merit grows,
Of one restrained no anger rises;
The good man puts aside base actions;
With lust and hate and illusion gone he has won Nirvāṇa.[1]

(*Mūlasarvāstivādin Vinaya*, Waldschmidt, p. 66;
Sutta-nipāta, I. 5.)

[1] This verse also occurs elsewhere in the Pāli.

XVIII. THE DEATH OF BUDDHA

THE canonical account of Buddha's death is a legend, which has become swollen to a great size owing to the insertion of discourses which were ascribed to the events of the last three months. Two such discourses are the sermon to Chunda in the previous chapter and the words to Subhadra given below.

BUDDHA, the Lord . . . with the congregation of his disciples dwelt at Kuśinagarī in the exercise-ground of the Mallas, in the grove of the twin śāl-trees. Then the Lord at the time of his attaining Nirvāṇa addressed Ānanda: "Prepare, Ānanda, for the Tathāgata between the twin śāl-trees a couch with its head to the north. To-day in the middle watch of the night the Tathāgata's attaining of Nirvāṇa with the element of Nirvāṇa that is without a remainder of rebirth will take place." " Even so, Reverend One," the elder Ānanda replied to the Lord, and having prepared a couch with its head to the north between the twin śāl-trees, came to the Lord, made obeisance with his head to the Lord's feet, and stood on one side. Standing there the elder Ānanda said to the Lord, " the couch, Reverend One, between the twin śāl-trees with its head to the north is prepared for the Tathāgata." Then the Lord went to the couch. Having gone he lay down on his right side, placing one foot on the other, aware of outer things, mindful and conscious, reflecting on the idea of Nirvāṇa.

Now at that time in Kuśinagarī a wanderer named Subhadra was dwelling, aged and venerable. He was a hundred and twenty years old, and was honoured, reverenced, respected, worshipped, and looked upon by the inhabitants of Kuśinagarī, the Mallas, as an arhat. He had heard that the ascetic Gautama in

THE DEATH OF BUDDHA

the middle watch of the night would attain Nirvāṇa there with the element of Nirvāṇa that is without a remainder of rebirth, and having a doubt about the doctrines he hoped that the Lord Gautama would be able to dispel his doubt. So having heard he left Kuśinagarī and came to the grove of twin śāl-trees.

At that time the elder Ānanda was walking up and down outside the vihāra on the promenade. Subhadra saw him from afar and approached him. On approaching him Subhadra exchanged courteous and pleasant greetings with him. Standing on one side Subhadra said to Ānanda, " I have heard, sir Ānanda, that the ascetic Gautama to-day in the middle watch of the night will attain Nirvāṇa with the element of Nirvāṇa that is without an element of rebirth. I have a doubt about the doctrines, and I have a hope that the Lord Gautama will be able to dispel my doubt. If it is not troublesome to sir Ānanda, we should like to enter and ask about a certain subject, if he would give the opportunity for explaining a question." [Ānanda refuses three times, and again Subhadra asks.]

Then the conversation with the elder Ānanda and Subhadra the wanderer was broken off. The Lord with his pure, divine hearing surpassing human hearing heard it, and he said to Ānanda, " Enough, Ānanda, do not prevent the wanderer Subhadra from entering and asking whatever he wishes. This will be my last conversation with wanderers of other schools, and he will be the last of my immediate disciples to enter the Order with the formula, ' Come, monk,' namely, Subhadra, the wanderer."

Then Subhadra on receiving the Lord's permission elated, pleased, and delighted, with extreme joy and happiness approached the Lord. Having approached he exchanged courteous and pleasant greetings with him and sat down at one side. Subhadra said to the Lord, " Those heretical schools in the common world, sir Gautama, such as Pūraṇa Kāśyapa, Maskarin Gośalīputra, Sañjaya Vairūṭīputra, Ajita Keśakambala, Kakuda Kātyāyana, and the Nirgrantha Jñātaputra professed to me his own profession. [There is a gap in the text here. From the Pāli we know that Subhadra asked if any of these teachers were successful in their professions, and Buddha tells him to let the question alone and hear what is essential for a true ascetic.]

> "At nine and twenty years of age, Subhadra,
> I left the world, my search for the good pursuing;
> Now fifty years and one year more are over,
> Since I went forth and left the world, Subhadra.
> Morality, concentration have I practised,
> And knowledge too with single mind attentive,
> Preaching the limits of the noble doctrine;
> Outside the range thereof is no ascetic."

"In whose doctrine and discipline, Subhadra, the noble Eightfold Way is not found, there no first ascetic is found, there no second, no third, no fourth ascetic is found. But in that doctrine and discipline in which the noble Eightfold Way is found, there the first ascetic is found, there the second, third, and fourth ascetic are found. In that doctrine and discipline, Subhadra, the noble Eightfold Way is found. Here the first ascetic is found, here the second, here the third, here the fourth. Outside thereof are no ascetics or brahmins. Void are other schools of ascetics or brahmins. Thus here in the congregation I roar the roar of the right assembly."

Now when this discourse on the doctrine was being spoken, the eye of the doctrine free from dust and free from stain arose in Subhadra the wanderer. So Subhadra having seen the doctrine, having attained the doctrine, and being plunged in the doctrine, with his doubts and perplexities gone, without being dependent on others, not led by others, but attaining

THE DEATH OF BUDDHA

confidence in the Master's teaching and doctrine, arose from his seat, and arranging his upper robe on one shoulder, approached Ānanda with folded hands and said to him, "Gain, reverend Ānanda, great gain is it that Ānanda has been consecrated by the Lord, the great teacher, with consecration as the pupil of the great teacher. To us also it would be gain, great gain, for us to receive in the well-spoken doctrine and discipline admission and ordination and the state of a monk." So the elder Ānanda said to the Lord, "This Subhadra, the wanderer, Lord, desires in the well spoken doctrine and discipline to receive admission and ordination and the state of a monk." Then the Lord addressed Subhadra the wanderer, "Come monk, practise the religious life." This was the elder's admission and ordination and state of a monk. [In the longer account other events of the last day are recorded, and finally Buddha's last words to the monks: "subject to decay are compound things; strive with earnestness."]

Then the Lord in the middle watch of the night attained Nirvāṇa with the element of Nirvāṇa that is without an element of rebirth.[1] At the moment that the Lord Buddha attained Nirvāṇa there was at that time a very violent earthquake and a fall of stars illuminating the quarters, and in the air the drums of the gods resounded. At the moment that the Lord Buddha attained Nirvāṇa both trees of the twin śāl-grove overspread the lion-couch of the Tathāgata with śāl-flowers. At the moment when the Lord attained Nirvāṇa a certain monk on that occasion uttered a verse:

Fair indeed are these noble trees of the sāla-grove;
When they have overspread with flowers the teacher who has won Nirvāṇa.

[1] The longer account records that Buddha attained the four trances (see Ch. V) and the five attainments.

At the moment that the Lord Buddha attained Nirvāṇa, Śakra, the Lord of gods, uttered a verse:

Impermanent verily are compounds, liable to arising and passing away;
For having arisen they cease; their quieting is bliss.

At the moment that the Lord Buddha attained Nirvāṇa, Brahmā Sahāmpati uttered a verse;

All beings in this universe shall lay aside their compound state;
Wherein such a teacher unrivalled in the worlds,
Who has attained a Tathāgata's powers, the seeing one, has won Nirvāṇa.

At the moment that the Lord Buddha attained Nirvāṇa the elder Aniruddha uttered verses:

> Stayed was the breathing in and out
> Of him with firm-established heart;
> Unmoving peace he has attained,
> The seeing one has won Nirvāṇa.
> Then was there a terrifying;
> Then was there a raising of hair;
> When he endowed with all the powers,
> The teacher reached his term of life.

> Then he with heart released from clinging
> Enduring the pains,
> As the extinction of a flame
> Even so was his heart's release.

Seven days after the Lord Buddha had attained Nirvāṇa the elder Ānanda making a circuit to the right round the Lord's funeral pyre, uttered a verse:

> With that jewel-body wherewith the Leader,
> He of great psychic power, went to the Brahma-world,
> Was he burnt with self-originating flame;
> With five hundred pairs of robes was he enwrapped.

For with as many as a thousand robes
Was the body of the Buddha enwrapped;
But therein two robes were not burnt,
The inner one, and also the outer one, the second.

(*Avadāna-śataka*, No. 40, 100.)

XIX. THE BODHISATTVA'S VOW

A BODHISATTVA is one who makes a vow not merely to win enlightenment but to become a Buddha. In Pāli Buddhism the doctrine appears late and we find it mentioned only with reference to the career of Gautama. It became popular with the avadānas of the Sarvāstivādins, and then of the first importance in the Mahāyāna, when it was taught that all beings are destined for the bodhisattva career.

A CERTAIN gardener went into Śrāvastī with a fresh lotus for king Prasenajit, and a lay-follower of the non-Buddhists saw him and asked him, "Are you selling this lotus?" He replied, "Yes." The man wanted to buy it, and then Anāthapiṇḍada came to the place. He offered double the price. They went on raising the price in turn up to 100,000. Then the gardener thought, "This Anāthapiṇḍada is a firm and a solid man, there must be some reason for it." As his doubt was raised, he asked the follower of the non-Buddhists why he was increasing the price. He said, "I do it for the sake of the Lord Nārāyaṇa," and Anāthapiṇḍada said, "I for the sake of the Lord Buddha." The gardener said, "who is he that is called Buddha?" Then Anāthapiṇḍada told him Buddha's qualities at length. The gardener said, "Householder, I myself will do honour to this Lord."

Then Anāthapiṇḍada went with the gardener to where the Lord was. The gardener saw the Lord Buddha adorned with the thirty-two marks of a great man and his limbs gleaming with the eighty minor marks, shining for a fathom round with a brilliance surpassing a thousand suns, and his gait like a mountain of gems fair all round. At the sight the gardener threw the lotus to the Lord, and as soon as thrown it expanded to the size of a cart-wheel and stayed above the Lord. So the gardener on seeing the miracle was like a tree cut down at the root, and falling at the Lord's feet made firm his purpose, and began to utter his vow: " Through this root of goodness, this rising of the thought, and this bestowal of a gift, may I become a Buddha in the blind world without leaders and guides, a taker across of beings who have not crossed, a releaser of the unreleased, a consoler of the unconsoled, and a leader to Nirvāṇa of those who have not attained Nirvāṇa." Then the Lord knowing the sequence of causes and the actions of the gardener displayed a smile. [Here follows a standing description of the smile of Buddha, when rays issue from his mouth, some going down to the hells, making the hot hells cool and the cold hells hot, others going through the heavens proclaiming impermanence, pain, voidness, and non-self.]

The Lord said, " Even so, Ānanda, even so. Not without a cause and occasion, Ānanda, do tathāgatas, arhats, perfect Buddhas display a smile. Do you see, Ānanda, that such worship has been done to me by that gardener in whom devotion has been aroused?" "Even so, Lord." "This gardener through that root of merit, that rising of the thought, and that bestowal of a gift, after attaining enlightenment pursued for three asankhyeyyas [1] of a cycle, having fulfilled the six perfections practised with great compassion, will become a fully enlightened Buddha named Padmottama endowed with the ten powers, the four confidences, the three special contemplations, and great compassion. This is his gift, which was his devotion to me."

(*Avadāna-Śataka*, No. 7.)

[1] Lit. "uncountables", used here probably of the four divisions of a cycle, the sinking to rest, the period of rest, the renewal of activity, and period of apparently steady activity.

XX. QUALITIES OF A BUDDHA

ALONG with the development of the idea of a bodhisattva as a being gradually acquiring more merits and perfections, went the conception of a Buddha as possessing ten powers. These are (1) knowledge of what is possible and impossible, (2) knowledge of the ripening of karmas, (3) of the destinies to which paths lead, (4) of the nature of the universe, (5) of the dispositions of individuals, (6) of their faculties, (7) of the purity or impurity of the trances and other attainments, (8) memory of his previous existences, (9) knowledge of the destinies of beings, (10) realization of the destruction of the āsavas. When Buddha was asked if he possessed complete knowledge and insight in the sense that knowledge was always present, he denied it, and said that he had the threefold knowledge, that is, the last three of the ten powers. Omniscience came to be attributed to Buddha in the sense that he was able to survey the world and bring any part of it within the net of his knowledge, as illustrated in this story.

BUDDHA the Lord . . . dwelt at Śrāvastī. In Śrāvastī a certain adulterer dwelt in evil ways. He was seized by the royal officers and brought before the king. Then the king condemned him as a criminal and sent him to be executed. The officers with black robes and drawn swords proclaiming his guilt led him bound with a garland of karavīra flowers about his neck through the streets, lanes, and cross-roads out through the south gate of the city.

Now there is nothing unknown, unseen, unperceived, or unrecognized by the Lord Buddhas. It is the rule that three times by night and three times by day the Lord Buddhas survey the world, and produce knowledge and insight, to see who is failing, who is progressing, who is wretched, who is in a difficulty, who is hindered, who is tending and inclining to a state of woe, whom can I draw from a state of woe, and set in heaven or release, to what man sunk in the mud of lusts may I hold out a hand, what man deprived of the noble treasures can I establish in the practice of the noble treasures, what roots of goodness, in whom they have not been made to grow, can I make to grow, in whom, when they have begun to grow, can I ripen them, and whom, in whom they are ripened, can I bring to release. And he said:

> The ocean, the abode of monsters,
> May even overpass its bounds;
> But ne'er does Buddha overpass
> The bounds of pupils to be trained.

So the Lord having robed himself early, took his bowl and robe and went into Śrāvastī for alms. The man saw the Lord Buddha adorned with the thirty-two marks of a great man and his limbs gleaming with the eighty minor marks, shining for a fathom round with a brilliance surpassing a thousand suns, and his gait like a mountain of gems fair all round, and on seeing the Lord he fell at his feet, and said, " O Lord, giver of boons, grant me dear life." Then the Lord said to the elder Ānanda, " Go to king Prasenajit, Ānanda, and say, ' give me this man, I will cause him to leave the world.' " So Ānanda went to king Prasenajit, and in the name of the Lord said, " give command, the Lord will cause this man to leave the world." The king approved and gave the command. The man was admitted by the Lord to the Order and ordained. As he practised, exerted himself, and strove, he saw the unsteady wheel of transmigration with its five divisions,[1] and rejecting the courses of all compound

---

[1] Life in heaven, as a man, as an animal, as a ghost, and in hell. A later division makes six by separating the heaven of the *asuras*, the rebel gods, as a separate career.

things whether by the law of cutting, falling, scattering, or dispersal, by riddance of all the depravities he realized arhatship. Having become an arhat he was free from passion for the three worlds, he became the same towards a clod of earth and gold, abiding with his mind the same towards space and the palm of his hand, with his knowledge like (cooling) sandalwood, and his ignorance like a broken eggshell, having acquired the (six) higher knowledges and the (four) branches of analysis, with his face turned against prosperity, gain, greed, and honour, to be worshipped, honoured, and praised by the gods with Indra and Upendra.[1]

(*Avadāna-śataka*, No. 18.)

---

[1] This description of an arhat occurs again and again in the avadānas, but the text is corrupt. It has been discussed by me in the *Indian Historical Quarterly*, 1941, p. 104.

XXI. BUDDHA AS SUPRAMUNDANE

THERE is nothing to show that the different schools ever tampered with what they held to be the Master's utterance. Any such action would have raised disputes, but we never find any wrangling about what actually is the Buddha-word. A distinction came to be made between the direct (or literal) meaning and the derived meaning, but even this shows that there was no wish to dispute the actual text. When we find novel doctrines appearing, such as the career of a bodhisattva in Sarvāstivādin texts, they are seen to occur in the birth-stories and avadānas, but never in the four Āgamas. Even the Lokottaravādins had no motive for doubting the text of the Buddha-word. They could accept all that was told of the Master's conduct as an ordinary man, because they held that he was then disguising his powers as Buddha and conforming to the custom of the world. The following declares itself as a poem, a eulogy which has been inserted in the *Mahāvastu* in order to expound the poet's favourite doctrine.

THE teaching of the leaders of men is held to be entirely supramundane; I will in truth set forth a eulogy of the best of sages.

When they have mastered the place and time and the ripening of their karma, and the truth has come to birth, the leaders teach the doctrine.

The Buddhas conform to the worldly practice of the world; even as they also conform to the supramundane teaching.

The supreme men show their four kinds of (human) conduct; yet weariness does not arise in those beings of good action.

They indeed wash their feet, though no dust clings to them; like lotus-petals are their feet. This is their conforming to the world.[1]

The Buddhas indeed bathe, though no taint is upon them, on their forms which are like gold. This . . .

They practise the washing of teeth and the lotus-scented mouth; they wear a dress and the threefold robe.

[1] This sentence is repeated below as a refrain.

The winds that blow their dress shake not their body, the dress of the lions of men. This . . .

They sit in the shade, but the sun's heat pains them not, the Buddhas that distil goodness. This . . .

Medicine they use, yet no sickness is found among them, a great fruit of the leaders. This . . .

Though able to ward off karma, the conquerors make a show of karma; they hide their sovereign power. This . . .

They take food indeed, but hunger pains them not, so that people may give them alms. This . . .

Water indeed they drink, but thirst pains them not; a marvel of the great sages is this. This . . .

Robes they wear, but the conqueror is ever dressed, and has the aspect of a god. This . . .

They grow hair, but no razor cuts it, their blue-black hair. This . . .

They show the marks of old age, but no old age is found in them, the conquerors with the conquerors' qualities. This . . .

Though they have performed the perfections for numberless crores of ages, they show the state of a beginner. This . . .

Without sexual union is the body of the Blessed One; yet they show a father and mother. This . . .

The Tathāgata, free from passion starting from Dīpankara, shows Rāhula as his son. This . . .

Though they have performed the perfection of wisdom for numberless crores of ages, they show the state of an infant. This . . .

They speak against false teachings in the world including the gods; yet again they visit those of other faiths. This . . .

Having become enlightened with unequalled enlightenment for the sake of all beings, they display a state of ease. This is their conforming to the world. (*Mahāvastu*, i. 168.)

INDEX

Abhidharma, 3, 9
Abhijñā, see Higher knowledges
Āgamas, 3, 85
Aggregates (mental elements, forms of will, etc.), 6, 33, 57, 58, 60, 61
Ajita, 76
Ājnātakauṇḍinya, 34, 58
Ānanda, 74 ff., 81, 83
Anāthapiṇḍada, 80
Aniruddha, 78
Anomiyā, 27
Arhat, Arhatship, 5, 43, 84
Āsavas, āsravas, see Corruptions
Asita, 18 ff., 23
Aśoka, 1, 44
Aśvaki, 34, 58
Ātman, see Self
Avadānas, 3, 8, 11
Āyatanas, 61

Benares, 34, 53, 58
Bhadraka, 34, 58
Birth-stories, see Jātakas
Blackie, 53 ff.
Boar's flesh, 70
Bodhisattva, 11, 13, 15, 22, 26, 29; career, 80; vow, 81
Brahmā, 16, 78
Brahmadatta, 63

Buddha, conception, 11; birth, 15, 19; four signs, 26; austerities, 29, 53; enlightenment, 29; last meal, 70; death, 1, 74 ff.; powers, 82; eye, 34; smile, 81; supramundane, 85; seven, 68
Buddha, private (one who does not preach), 5

Chain of causation, 29, 31 ff.
Chandaka, 26 ff.
Chunda, 70; discourse, 71
Corruptions, āsavas, 7, 53, 59; three, 29; four, 33, 82
Cycles, 4, 31, 81

Dhammapada, 3
Dhātus, 61
Dīpankara, 86
Dīrgha-āgama, 3
Disciples, five, 4, 34, 57 ff.
Divine eye, 17, 29, 30, 53
Doctrine, 5, 69

Ekottarika-āgama, 3
Enlightenment, 29 ff., 37
Entering the stream, 5, 48

INDEX

Fast-day vows, 11 ; rules, 38
Formula of welfare (Jewel discourse), 65

Gautama, a sage, 53
Gautama, Gotama, Buddha's clan-name, 15, 63, 67
Ghaṭikāra, 22
Groups, skandhas, five, 6, 7, 36, 57, 61
Guptika, 60 ff.

Higher knowledges, 53, 64, 84

Jains (Nirgranthas), 4, 76
Jātakas, 3, 49, 53, 63

Kalpas, see Cycles
Kampilla, 63
Kanthaka, 26 ff.
Kapilavastu, Kapilavatthu, 19, 27, 28
Karma, 4, 30, 55, 60, 61, 85
Kāśī, 49 ff., 53
King who would not fight, 49
Kośala, 49 ff.
Kuśinagarī, 5, 74

Lalitavistara, 11
Laymen, 7 ; five rules, 38 ; fast-day rules, 38
Licchavis, 63
Lokottaravādins, 9, 11, 85
Lumbinī, 15

Madhyama-āgama, 3

Mahānāman, 34, 58, 59
Mahāprajāpatī, 22, 27
Mahāsanghikas, 3, 9
Mahāvastu, 3, 11, docetic, 26
Mahāyāna, 9, 11, 80
Mallas, 74
Māra, 29, 34
Maskarin Gośālīputra, 76
Mathurā, 44, 48
Maudgalyāyana, 39
Māyā, 11 ff.
Memory of past existences, 30, 53
Middle path, 35
Mṛigī, 25

Nālaka, 18
Nirgranthas, see Jains
Nirvāna, 4, 5, 7, 20, 24, 35, 41, 42, 48, 57, 60, 71, 74, 77
Non-returner, 5, 48
Non-self, 7 ; marks of, 57, 60
Novices, ten rules, 38

Once-returner, 5
Order, 48, 66 ff.
Ordination, 38, 77
Outer way, 18, 53, 63

Padmottama, 81
Pānchāla, 63
Pāragā, 53, 56
Paths, see Way ; ten, 8
Peliyaksha, 54
Piṭakas, see Scriptures
Prasenajit, 80, 83

INDEX

Psychic powers, 53, 69, 78
Pūraṇa Kāśyapa, 76
Pūrṇa, 40 ff.

Rāhula, 26, 38, 86
Rakshita, 63, 64
Rebirth, 4, 67
Refuges, 5, 38, 43, 48
Renunciation, 26 ff.
Rishipatana, Rishivadana, 34, 35, 58

Śakra, 16, 27, 78
Samyukta-āgama, 3
Sañjaya, 76
Sankhāras, volitional activities of the self, *see* Aggregates
Śāriputra, 38
Sarvāstivādins, 3, 70, 80; doctrine, 5, 8
Schools, 8, 85
Scriptures, 2 ff.
Self, five groups, 6, 57; brahmin theory, 7
Siddhārtha, 22
Signs, four, 22
Simeon, 18
Skandhas, *see* Groups
Śrāvastī, 42, 82, 83
Sroṇāparāntakas, 41, 42

Subhadra, 74 ff.
Śuddhodana, 12 ff., 19, 20, 27, 28
Sūtra, 3

Tathāgata, 35, 48, 78
Topknot-festival, 27
Trance, 18; four, 29, 53, 77
Tree of Enlightenment, Bodhi-tree, 29, 34
Tripiṭaka, *see* Scriptures
Truths, four, 5, 34, 36
Truth-utterance, 53, 56
Tushita, 11, 26

Ujjenī, 18
Undetermined questions, 6, 7
Universal king, 14, 22
Upagupta, 40, 44 ff.

Vaiśālī, 63, 64
Vāsavadattā, 40, 44 ff.
Vāshpa, 34, 58, 59
Vasishṭha, 27; Vāsishṭhas, 63
Vinaya, 2
Vindhyas, 18
Void, 9

Way, eightfold, 5, 34 ff., 76; four stages, 5, 65; outer, 18, 53, 63

The titles below are available in the Wisdom of the East Series. All are presented in heirloom-quality sewn, cloth bindings and are printed on acid-free paper. To order, if not available at your local bookseller, please phone toll-free 800-526-2778, or write: Charles E. Tuttle Company, Inc., P.O. Box 410, Rutland, VT 05702-0410

The Book of Mencius (abridged) translated from the Chinese by Lionel Giles (0-8048-1844-4)

A Confucian Notebook by Edward Herbert (0-8048-1793-6)

The Dhammapada: Sayings of Buddha translated from the Pali with notes by Narada Thera (0-8048-1845-2)

The Hymns of Zarathustra: Being a Translation of the Gathas with introduction and commentary by Jacques Duchesne-Guillemin (0-8048-1810-X)

Manifold Unity: The Ancient World's Perception of the Divine Pattern of Harmony and Compassion by Collum (0-8048-1811-8)

The Message of Islam: Being a Resume of the Teaching of the Qur-an: With Special References to the Spiritual and Moral Struggles of the Human Soul by A. Yusuf Ali (0-8048-1794-4)

The Perfection of Wisdom: The Career of the Predestined Buddhas: A Selection of Mahayana Scriptures translated from the Sanskrit by E.J. Thomas (0-8048-1795-2)

The Quest of Enlightenment: A Selection of the Buddhist Scriptures translated from the Sanskrit by E.J. Thomas (0-8048-1846-0)

The Road to Nirvana: A Selection of the Buddhist Scriptures translated from the Pali by E.J. Thomas (0-8048-1796-0)

The Sayings of Confucius: A New Translation of the Greater Part of the Confucian Analects by Lionel Giles (0-8048-1847-9)

The Sayings of Muhammad by Allama Sir Abdullah Al-Mamun Al-Suhrawardy (0-8048-1797-9)

The Song of the Lord: Bhagavadgita by E.J. Thomas (0-8048-1812-6)

The Spirit of Zen: A Way of Life, Work and Art in the Far East (2nd edition) by Alan W. Watts (0-8048-1798-7)

Tao Te Ching: The Book of the Way and Its Virtue by J.J.L. Duyvendak (0-8048-1813-4)

STAFFORD LIBRARY
COLUMBIA COLLEGE
1001 ROGERS STREET
COLUMBIA, MO 65216